# HOUSE OF GRACE

Big sinners raising little sinners

# MICHAEL DIMARCO

Hungry
Planet

First Edition: February 2015
Cover and interior design by Hungry Planet.
For booking and media information visit: www.hungryplanet.net

ISBN: 9780986134906

10 9 8 7 6 5 4 3 2 1

# CONTENTS

WWW.GRACECITY.ORG

# PROLOGUE

**WRITING THIS BOOK WAS SCARY.** It's scary to write a book on a subject when most wouldn't view you as a typical expert. It's also scary to share your views when you think that the establishment, in this case the church, has missed the mark in helping parents disciple their kids.

In fact, reading this book may be scary for you. You and I need to form a contract of some sort before you begin. We need to agree that parenting is more an art than a science. Every child is different as is every parent and family unit. Because of this, you need to know my heart in writing this book; I want to start a conversation within our faith families that asks the question, in light of the gospel, "isn't it time that our theology of parenting grows up, that the primary reason to parent is to build upon and promote gospel growth?" Having this conversation means that, as you read, you may feel uneasy as I

1

describe a parenting style or philosophy. Maybe it applies to you more than you like? Or maybe you're fine with it and I am making it less beneficial or biblical? It's going to be uncomfortable. I am here to tell you that our parenting needs more grace. And grace will be extended to you from me as well. I've messed up in the past and I'll mess up in the future. But my prayer is that, as you read this book, you will measure everything against what you know of the gospel and beckon the Holy Spirit to work through this book and, perhaps, in spite of it.

Before you consider any parenting advice from any source, whether it's secular, religious, academic, or anecdotal, it is important you know the person's beliefs on the purpose of parenting. After all, the purpose is the ultimate goal of a thing. So if your goal and the expert's goal differ, then taking their advice would be nonsensical. In the end, if you followed all of their advice, you would have built a relationship with your child that you didn't want to create and grow them in a direction you didn't want them to grow. With that in mind, it may seem strange that you have to wait three chapters until you get to *The Purpose of Parenting*. So, I suggest that you consider the purpose of parenting for yourself. Is the ultimate end to your child rearing to create an emotionally happy and/or physically healthy child? Or do you have your sights set on developing a deferential and subservient child? There are some whose main goal is to just get through the teen years without rebellion or to come through with an adult child that is a friend as well. Let me just say this: I have not raised a child into adulthood or completed an exhaustive scientific study on parenting or early childhood development. That's not my purpose or the purpose of this book. I want this book to address parenting through the lens and filter of the gospel. And that means that I will be addressing some sacred cows of parenting that most of us believe to be biblical but very well may not be.

Whatever you have imagined your goal to be up until now, let me suggest one more (and this is a spoiler alert for chapter four.) This goal is meant for those who believe in the gospel of Jesus Christ; for those of us who have surrendered our lives to Christ and live to serve him, we know that everything in our lives is meant to bring God glory, including our relationships with our children. When the scientific/academic community gives parenting advice based on measuring human behavior without acknowledging the human condition (sin), they are giving advice founded on a humanistic gospel. For the Christian, if parenting advice is not rooted in the aim of making disciples and glorifying God, it must be considered incomplete, even suspect. Usually, the advice will be nothing more than behavior modification, an elevation of "self", or a prescription to enable the parent to maintain a pre-parent lifestyle as much as possible. So the purpose of this book is to present the argument that the ultimate purpose of parenting is rooted in the Great Commission and that purpose is discipleship. Not merely a conversion prayer at our child's bedside, but a lifelong relationship of discipling our children and letting them experience who God is and who we are with and without him. Thus, every parenting decision (and the advice we give and take on parenting) needs to be built on discipleship. Discipleship, rooted in the Great Commission, is the foundation for a house of grace.

"And Jesus came and said to them, 'All authority in heaven and on earth has been given to me. Go therefore and make disciples of all nations, baptizing them in the name of the Father and of the Son and of the Holy Spirit, teaching them to observe all that I have commanded you. And behold, I am with you always, to the end of the age.'"

— Matthew 28:18-20

# INTRODUCTION—
# A CULTURE OF CONFESSION

*"Unless the Lord builds the house, those who build it labor in vain. Unless the Lord watches over the city, the watchman stays awake in vain." - Psalm 127:1*

MY WIFE AND I GREW UP IN TWO VERY DIFFERENT FAMILIES. I'm Italian and Irish, so sharing my feelings is not a problem, and I'm not very quiet. My wife grew up in a Norwegian household where they never talked about their feelings, and ignoring differences was the order of the day. As a result, when Hayley would accidentally step on my foot, which was more often than you think for my self-proclaimed and adorable klutz, she wouldn't say "Sorry," she'd say, "What was your foot doing there?" In Hayley's family, there was never any accepting responsibility, or apologizing for even the littlest of things, nor any discussion beyond "Duh, keep your foot out of my way." This meant that when she stepped on my foot, her first thought wasn't to apologize. Her first thought was to deflect. I, on the other hand, was raised by a veteran of World War II and the Korean War, so if something was broken in our house there was immediate interrogations until we found out how it broke and who broke it. With six kids, there were a lot of fingers to point but thankfully my dad was too gentle for water boarding! Because of this grand inquisition style of parenting, you would think that I would have learned how to face up to the consequences of mistakes and accept responsibility. Instead, I mainly learned how to lie about my involvement, lawyer-up, or be prosecutor and judge bent on delivering swift justice.

Neither of us had been raised in homes where the gospel was central. Neither of us had been taught what it means to live a life of faith, especially in relationship to raising kids. So as soon as we got pregnant, we knew that some things needed to be changed in our family tree, from the roots up. Together we set about the project of reverse engineering the branches down to the trunk.

### Rewarding Confession

A few years back, my wife was discipling some college women and she was going to have some girls over for a dance party (or rhythmic movement party, depending on your denomination) using the Xbox. So, right before they arrived I fired up the Kinect sensor bar that would allow them to play and found that the motor was busted. At this point, in my childhood household, we would start interrogations and separate the witnesses so we could get a speedy conviction. But because Hayley and I had prepared for moments like this we had a different plan of action. Our daughter, who was four at the time, was sitting at her play table nearby coloring. So I said, "you know what

Hayley, the Kinect is broken. Maybe it broke when I installed the new DVD player last week. I'm sorry but it doesn't work." I decided to share the possibility of it being my responsibility, although I was fairly certain it wasn't me. After a pause, my daughter said, "Boppa? If a ball hit that...*would that have broken it?*" With my back to her, I grinned big, and said, "Well, it depends on the size of the ball and how fast the ball was traveling." So she said, "well, I was playing volleyball with this ball..." and then I really grinned because I used to play and coach volleyball at the university level. She continued, "I didn't say anything because it didn't look broken, just knocked over." So I went over to her and hugged her and said, "Thank you so much for telling me. Now I don't have to wonder what happened. Let's go to the game store and maybe we can buy a used Kinect so Momma can have her party and we'll go get ice cream on the way." So Addy and I climbed into my truck and we gave thanks that we could afford to replace the broken part. I praised her for searching her heart and her memory for the possibility that she was responsible and, most importantly, for sharing that possibility with me. That's why we were getting ice cream: *to celebrate and reward her confession.* Not only that, we talked about sin. We talked about what it is that makes us want to hide like Adam and Even when we've messed up, why confession is so important, and how it's evidence that God is working in our hearts.

This style of parenting has been the rule of thumb for our household and now our daughter confesses effortlessly, all because we reward confession. She has come to see the value that confession has over concealment, and because of that, we have lots of opportunities to teach her and to share with her the grace of God. Much of what you read in this book came from reverse engineering our family trees but also the trends in families throughout the Western church.

We started the process with research from Barna and LifeWay. We found that 65 - 75% of kids that grow up in the church, by the time they're in their mid-twenties, will have left the church. That statistic bothered us greatly. "What's at the root," we asked ourselves, "of this exodus? How do we prodigal-proof our own home?"

In an attempt to do just that, we decided that the first step in this process for us was having free unfettered access to her heart and mind so that we could help her to know God. We desperately wanted to create a home where our daughter would feel safe to share her life with us, where she wouldn't have to pretend until she moved out and could finally be herself. As we thought about how to reverse engineer such a transparent relationship, we decided that the first thing we had to do was create a culture of confession in our home. I'll get into that more later, but let me just say that this idea of confession fundamentally changes the way families interact with one another and with the sin in their lives.

The next thing learned from working with teens on the precipice of rejecting their parents' faith was the importance of helping our daughter to make her faith her own. All of us raised in Christian homes start out with a borrowed faith. We believe whatever our parents tell us, and that means that we decide who God is based on who our parents are and who they say he is. But as we grow, this borrowed or symbiotic faith has to grow into a faith of our own that can stand on its own. We knew that we had to not only *tell* her what we believed, but *show* her what we believed. We knew we had to learn, now more than ever, to act upon our faith so that those little eyes that were always observing us would see consistency between what we said and what we did. Hypocrisy was not an option for us, at least unconfessed hypocrisy. But if we were willing to acknowledge those lapses in sanity where we had preached one thing and had done another, then our contrite confession of failure would make our faith more appealing to our child. So we began to create a parenting philosophy based on reverse engineering what we knew about the majority of Christian young people struggling with the faith of their parents.

## The Importance of Confession

In fact, if I could choose one thing to change about our Christian communities it would be to increase confession. I think this has a direct correlation to the drop out rate and to changing that statistic across the board. I don't think it's about the music we are playing at church or how relevant the communication style is. If kids see unconfessed hypocrisy in their parents and church, why should they want to stay? Hypocrisy is the least attractive and effective way to encourage someone to do what we want them to do.

A.W. Tozer once said, "Christ can and will save a man who has been dishonest, but he cannot save him while he's dishonest." Confession requires honesty, and faith requires confession. So, spiritually healthy children require healthy opportunities to confess in a safe environment. Without it they will go looking for the safest place where they can be themselves. So let me ask you, what is safer: to confess your mistakes in a bar or in a church? What about in a public university or Bible college? Is it safer for your child to confess in your living room or in their first college dorm room? How we answer these questions reveals the chances of our children leaving the church in search of a safer haven for the mistakes they have made and will make.

When my wife Hayley and I married, we didn't plan on having kids unless we adopted. So you can imagine our surprise when we found out we were pregnant. While the idea of parenting was new to us, we knew we wanted our family to look different than the ones we grew up in, so we sat down and started to discuss our family trees and how we were going to raise a daughter that we had spent little time preparing for. Over the next nine months we started to reverse engineer all of the issues that we had seen with teenagers through our writing, speaking, and ministry to teens and their parents. Two of the questions we kept coming back to were "Why do so many young people leave the church and leave the faith by the time they hit their early twenties?" and "Would it be possible for us to prodigal-proof our home so that our daughter wouldn't be a part of this statistic?"

As I looked around for confirmation of our thinking, I found that almost every conversation, sermon, or blog post I consumed emphasized an authoritarian sort of approach to child rearing. Which led me to search out if there were any other possibilities besides the encouraged authoritarian or the "devilish" permissive models. What I found was that researchers have identified essentially four types of parents. Of course these researchers didn't look at families through the filter of faith, so that's exactly what we did.

Now before I go any further, let me say for myself what C.S. Lewis said in the introduction to his book "Reflection on the Psalms", when he said, "I write for the unlearned about things in which I am unlearned myself. It often happens that two schoolboys can solve difficulties in their work for one another better than the master can. The fellow-pupil can help more than the master because he knows less. The difficulty we want him to explain is one he has recently met. The expert met it so long ago that he has forgotten it. He sees the whole subject, by now, in such a different light that he cannot conceive what is really troubling the pupil; he sees a dozen other difficulties which ought to be troubling him but aren't."

I quote and echo that so that if there is a time when I sound authoritative or instructive in word or tone, it is not because I hold myself as an expert in this area, but because this schoolboy (in parenting) has very possibly seen the light and has a passion to share it with you, my fellow or future parents. I only hope that what I have to say from the scripture I have studied, the experiences I have had, and the relationships I have observed and walked through, will help lead your family deeper into faith and into building a house of grace.

The truth is that confession, while uncomfortable, is good for us all. When we are free to confess we are authentic. Confession keeps you from being fake, from hiding and from living a double life. I have seen so many teens that are one way with their parents and as soon as they are away from prying eyes they are completely different. My wife ministers to thousands of young women and we're always amazed at how many girls conceal their fear, worry and pain as they cut, purge and starve themselves to death. When we ask them to share with their parents, they tell us they are too afraid of what will happen if they do. Confession, for them, is not rewarded but punished, which is such a tragedy because confession is the only thing that truly keeps us from leading a double life. That is because when we are transparent and honest, we don't have a need to hide things and attempt to avoid detection from those who love us.

We were made to confess. Confession isn't dangerous; it doesn't damage us in a negative way, it damages us in a positive way. Confession doesn't damage what is holy in us; it damages what is sinful. Confession just confirms God's Word by agreeing with him that we are imperfect (see Romans 3:10). It allows us to say "I was 'that' but because of God's grace I'm now 'this.'"

Confession isn't only for the confessor. Confession also prevents others from believing they have to be perfect in order to follow Christ. It makes your testimony about your salvation wholly true. When you go to court and you have to testify, you testify to "tell the truth, the whole truth, and nothing but the truth." That's because a half-truth is a whole lie. When you confess you don't keep back some of your testimony in secret, but you make your testimony wholly true by being free to confess just who you truly are, a sinner saved by grace. This truth helps others to see that he loved them while they were still sinners.

Confession has a bad rap and it has it for a good reason. Confession can be dangerous to your image. When you confess you can lose respect instantly. Being human, it's easy to judge people who reveal their failures and blemishes to us. With certain confessions, you might just lose your position, leadership, or even your favorite son/daughter status. Confession can be dangerous to those positions given to us by man, because it shines a light on our sin. When you confess, you might not only lose your position but you might even lose some relationships.

It's human nature to reason that there are some things people just don't want to hear about how sinful you've been. We all know those things that we fear hearing from those we love. Each of us knows the one confession we never want to hear from our spouse, best friend, or teenager. So, out of the fear of hearing the worst, we tend to figuratively plug our ears and hum loudly so we don't have to hear the absolute worst thing we could hear. When we attempt to avoid these kinds of disastrous confessions in our homes and even church communities, we subconsciously teach sin concealment and sin avoidance rather than confession. In the process we create communities founded on hypocrisy rather than faithfulness, and deceit rather than honesty. It's a big reason why our kids are deserting the faith when they move out of our homes.

The answer to this hypocritical tendency is for all of us to begin to concentrate on teaching our kids not to hide their sin, but teaching them how to rebound from sin. If you know anything about the gospel then you know that we all have sinned, will sin, and are probably sinning right now in ways we are not even aware of yet. Sin is an unavoidable fact of human nature. So if we know this about ourselves *and* our kids, shouldn't we then teach our kids and one another how to rebound from sin so that we won't be drug down deeper into it as we try to hide our mess? So that we don't deceive others into thinking that they are somehow inferior because they aren't perfect like us? Author and pastor Bill Clem was the first I heard talk about sin rebound. In his book *Disciple: Getting Your Identity in Jesus*, he talks about how Jesus demonstrated this discipleship method in his relationship with Peter:

"Jesus warned Peter that he was going to be spiritually attacked. One of the most amazing things about these verses is that Jesus prayed for Peter's faith and for his recovery after it failed. I get so busy praying that I and the people I care about will not sin, that I do not pray for a resilient faith and a God-honoring rebound from sin. Peter responds to Jesus with a prideful swagger, pledging to follow unwaveringly to prison and to death. Perhaps Peter was implying that he would follow even if no one else in the community did. Jesus called Peter to community thinking again by saying, "When you have turned again, strengthen your brothers (v. 32). The opposite of community thinking is competitive thinking."[i]

Ultimately, the prescription for building a culture of sin rebound is found in James 5:16 where it says, "confess your sins to one another and pray for one another so that you may be healed. The prayer of a righteous person has great power as it is working." When we confess to God, what I call vertical confession, we receive forgiveness from God (as seen in 1 John 1:9). But God is telling us here in James, that when we confess to one another (horizontal confession) we receive healing. Confession in both directions is necessary for our spiritual and emotional health. This idea of healing speaks to the fact that the sins that consume us, control us, and hurt us, are healed only once they are confessed to another brother or sister in Christ. So, when our kids don't have someone to confess to at home, when and where do they receive the healing that James is talking about?

James 5:16 emphasizes the exchange that takes place in the use of "one another." The use of "one another" means that we both hear confessions and make our own, rather than just being a hearer alone. My mom wanted me to grow up to be the Pope, but I liked girls too much, so the next best thing I could do to hear confessions all day and dispense wisdom was to work as a bartender. It's how I paid for college. Like me, you may be good at hearing confessions, but if you never offer any of your own then the healing is incomplete. We are meant to be honest about our own sinfulness and to share in the humanity of our children. But we are not meant to be dumpers, who make ourselves and our failures the continual topic of conversation, telling all of our sins to everyone we see while never listening to the struggles of others.

James also describes the people we are to confess our sins to as righteous. That doesn't mean perfect, it doesn't contradict Romans 3:10, which says there are no righteous, people at all, because in this instance righteous means a spiritually mature person. Spiritually mature doesn't simply mean pastor or elder, because from sin to sin, some people are more mature in certain areas than others. You can have a godly man or woman who can give great spiritual counsel about everything but the one thing you need to confess, and so in this instance they are not the righteous person you need. Because of their experiences they might flip out over what you have to say rather than offer you God's grace. This is *exactly* why our kids so often fear confessing to us, because we are not spiritually mature enough to handle what they have to confess. But instead we flip out as we allow worry, regret, resentment, shame, and fear take precedent over forgiveness and healing.

Your kids know you from experience; they know your flip-out meter. So when they are looking for a righteous person to confess to, they might not come to you because they don't want you to freak out.

So, in those instances, you would not be a righteous person for them to confess to. Tragically, a lot of times mom and dad are not righteous in the areas that kids need to talk about the most. So we have youth pastors on speed dial that can tell us what they've heard from our kids (and then we can flip out). But this kind of parenting only breeds distance between our kids and ourselves and teaches them that hiding (sin concealment) is far better than coming clean.

Police officers, firemen, EMTs and other first responders are taught how to handle worst-case scenarios. Firemen don't spend all of their time on preventative Smokey the Bear educational stuff: they train how to quickly and unemotionally respond to the worst-case scenario, a raging inferno. A police officer, for a routine traffic stop, is running through the protocol for the worst-case scenario. That's why when they approach your mini-van with the Jesus fish and stick figures on the back, their hand is on their gun and they treat you like a potential threat. In the same way, the EMT doesn't show up on the scene with only Band-Aids and Bactine, ill prepared without everything they need to resuscitate someone whose heart has stopped.

As the God-ordained first responder in your child's life, how have you been training for those worst-case scenario confessions? Most of us would say not at all, because we don't want to hear them. So, we spend all our time teaching sin avoidance and punishing confession, essentially and tragically reinforcing sin concealment.

In order to be the first responder that your child calls in the case of a spiritual emergency, you have to become for them a righteous person. This means that when they confess to you, you cannot flip out and take their sin as an attack on your parenting skills, or treat their confession like a parole hearing for a third-strike offender. In a family that wants true confession, the kind that brings a spirit of repentance, confession has to be rewarded. If that kind of confession is punished, then any incentive for future confession is gone and your kids go back into deception mode. But in a house of grace we don't punish confession. Just like God offers instant forgiveness for sin, so do we. This can seem daunting so I suggest that you look for opportunities in the small things, where it doesn't hurt and freak you out, where you have spiritual maturity and can appreciate the confession and then talk about our sin nature that we inherited from our first parents.

The truth is that Satan wants us feeling alone and unable to be ourselves. He wants isolation, because with that there is no healing. The top two causes of death among teens are unforeseen accidents and suicide. And the number one reason people commit suicide is because they feel alone and hopeless; they have nowhere to go for healing and acceptance as a less than perfect sinner.

For people who have lived life hard before they had kids, like my wife and I, the enemy says, "Don't share that with your daughter. Keep your past sins hidden so they won't follow in your footsteps," but hidden sin isn't fully redeemed until it is used to bring glory to God. Your sin glorifies God when you confess, repent and then allow others to learn from the amazing grace that God has given you, displaying how amazing God truly is. If you have had no need for his grace then why would your children want it? If they don't want his grace then they don't need his Son.

We should all have homes that feel like the home of the prodigal son, where our children can come home and they aren't greeted with lectures but with understanding, compassion, grace, and a sprinting parent's embrace. Unfortunately, our natural bent is to parent more like the elder brother than the father. The elder brother disowns the younger, saying to the father, "But this son of yours..." Yet the father never disowns the rebel child. When the rebel child returns home, the elder brother brings a lecture, but the father throws the confessing son a party. So, too, should we celebrate the confessions of our sons and daughters, especially when remembering that we are just as sinful as they are. We are all prodigals parenting prodigals. Big sinners raising little sinners.

The truth is that most of us within the Christian church have either adopted a humanistic gospel of parenting (wanting our children to be educated, moral, well-mannered, and good citizens) or a prosperity gospel of parenting (wanting our kids to have a better life than we had); both are false gospels. The prosperity gospel of parenting is frighteningly prevalent and dangerous because God might have a different plan for your children. He might allow them to walk through a terrible mistake so they can be in a place where you never wanted them to be but God needed them to be. Thinking this way allows you to hear their confessions without freaking out. Trusting God with even the sin in their lives is the best thing you can do for your child. After all, it's sin that gives us access to the saving grace of Jesus Christ. So why would we want to pretend like our kids have none, and instead turn a blind eye to the very nature of their souls: sinners saved by grace?

In my early thirties, I got arrested for theft when I was caught "borrowing" petty cash and pawning items from my work so that I could gamble in-between paychecks. After I got paid, I would replace the money and get the items out of pawn and return them to work. It all got exposed because one day, at a blackjack table, I said this prayer, "God, I'm sick of this! Please get me out of it!" Later that day, a co-worker found what I had been doing for a year and a half, and he asked me, "What's the deal?" I confessed right then and there. I lost my job and, a short time later, I was arrested. While I sat in my holding cell at the local county jail, I saw a tattered old Gideon Bible, and I said, "God this is such a cliché! So let me take this all the way." And while I don't recommend this, I closed my eyes, flipped open the Bible and pointed at the page, and by God's grace my finger landed on 2 Corinthians 5:17, "Therefore if any man is in Christ he's a new

ng to build a c

creation, the old has passed away, behold the new has come." Right there I surrendered my life. If it weren't for the confession that led to that jail cell, I wouldn't be here today. After many failed job interviews where I freely offered my confession of why I left my last job, I finally gained employment with Logos Bible Software (now called Faithlife), the largest Bible software company in the world, where I told my testimony, and their response was "We've heard worse," and they hired me. "What kind of people work here?!", I thought to myself. But because of this kind of grace I started traveling and speaking, teaching people how to study God's Word. I spoke at seminaries teaching Bible scholars how to go deeper into Greek and Hebrew, I met my wife Hayley, and my writing ministry exploded, all out of that one confession. And yes, my daughter knows this story.

In order to build a culture of confession, we must begin to adore and celebrate the confessions of our children rather than fear them. We have to be prepared for the worst-case sins that may never be confessed. We've got to prepare ourselves to make our first response an appreciation that their spirits have been sensitive enough to feel the tug of conviction and the promptings of the Spirit. In our household, when our daughter confesses something to us we smile, hug her, and say "thank you for telling me that." We point out that the very Spirit of God is evident and active in her life and that her confession is evidence that God is moving and at work. What a joy to celebrate! Then we talk to her sinner-to-sinner about why we sin and how much God loves us in spite of it. We remind her that confession is the first step to forgiveness from the Father and the beginning of the change and the rebound of repentance and healing from confessing to one another. When we receive her confessions with grace, love, and even joy, we create in our child a desire for transparency, not secrecy, for communication, not concealment. This allows us to build, brick-by-brick, a strong and safe home-life for our child that is a sanctuary of healing in the battles of life, where we become her first choice for confession and guidance because of the healing and rebounding we provide.

So if we are to build a house of grace, consider confession to be the front door: always unlocked, always open. But before we hang the door, we've got some digging and foundation work to do; we have to lay the foundation. We have to ask and answer the question, in light of the gospel, "What is the purpose of parenting?" That's the subject of the next chapter. But before we go there, I've included at the end of each chapter questions I've received at my House of Grace weekend events from parents in attendance that I thought might be on your mind as well.

* * *

### "Yes, grace but..." - Questions from a Reader

Q: *"Isn't it just encouraging their sin when you reward their confession?"*

The same could be said of God sending His Son to die for our sins: "Isn't God's grace and forgiveness just encouraging us to sin more?" I can imagine onlookers at the crucifixion responding similarly when they heard Jesus telling one of the thieves that he would see him in paradise: "How can he offer forgiveness so fast? Doesn't that just encourage a life of thievery?"

Celebrating confession is not synonymous with celebrating sin. When we celebrate confession we celebrate that the Holy Spirit is doing a work in their life. We celebrate the fact that they are telling the truth, that they are becoming truth tellers. Celebration of confession is a celebration of open dialogue and a life lived in the light, instead of in darkness, concealment, and shame.

When you see their confession as an opportunity for discipleship, you are prepared to share the gospel with your child as you talk about why disobedience is so natural to us, and what it is in our sin nature that makes us want to sin. Living under this same gospel truth, you can then empathize with their sinful heart because you are just the same. Then you can include them in the process of changing their behavior and outlook.

These moments are important when your focus is living in the light rather than simply modifying behavior. Because when your child lives in the light, then discipleship discussions about disobedience can continue in an open dialogue. But when confession is immediately punished, it closes conversation and creates an atmosphere where kids would rather stay in darkness than talk about their sin nature.

Celebrating confession sounds dangerous to a parent that doesn't finish the celebration with discipleship. But on the contrary, not celebrating it is more dangerous. Celebration is the safety mechanism that allows the parent to disciple out of the gospel of grace, instead of punish out of the raw emotion of our desire for justice and performance. As we celebrate confession we take a pause, a selah, that allows us to appreciate the gospel truths before moving into discipleship.

While the rest of the world might never reward the confession of your child the way you do, as you explain this idea to them you create a deeper bond of love, grace and healing between you and your child, and that is invaluable, especially as your child enters their teen and college years. Immediate punishment doesn't heal the sins of your child. While it might correct the behavior or make the offended party feel better, it will only serve to reinforce their living in the dark. Celebrating confession turns on the lights and encourages transparency between you and your child.

*Q: When you confess your possible fault in the mistakes and even sins of your child, isn't that just teaching her that they are ultimately responsible for other people's sin? Surely you don't want to teach your child that it is their fault when someone else sins against them, such as physical or emotional abuse.*

You should never apologize for your child's sin, but look for opportunities to examine your own culpability in overlooking or ignoring the shepherding of your child in each situation. Examining your own heart makes you quick to look for ways you might be responsible and so makes you slow to accuse and assign blame and quick to nurture and empathize. This allows cooler heads to prevail and shepherding and mentoring to take place; rooted in love, instead of correction and performance. Even when it's obvious that what she did was certainly her fault, you can still look for ways you might have contributed to her failure, but then (shoulder-to-shoulder) sit with her and shepherd her through the aftermath which inevitably includes her actions or inactions that caused it. But because you've done the initial self-examination and sharing, you are seen as an ally and veteran teammate on her life's journey instead of a judge and jury. In all of this, your child may well learn by observation, but observation isn't a command to do the same.

With regards to physical abuse, one of the reasons we don't spank is because we have instructed our daughter that it's never ok for anyone to hit her in any situation or for any reason, even if that person says they're doing it because they love her or that her actions "deserve" it. Teaching your child by example, that hitting is never acceptable, is far more efficient than avoiding self-examination in the fear that she will begin to accept blame for the sins of others.

*Q: If everyone is a teammate, and no one is the coach, who is in charge? While I want my children to know that I am on their side, I think that we are on the same team, but we are not equals or peers. I would disciple my peer much differently than I would my child. A coach is not equal to the player.*

"Big sinners raising little sinners" is all about being equals. That means our hearts are equally as sinful and undeserving of mercy and grace, yet God offers it through his son anyway. Paul says we are all running a race; the parent does not stop running once they become a parent, they just have a newborn to slow them down! In the area of discipleship, a sports team analogy with coach and player is not a sufficient one, but a better example of discipleship would be a mountain climbing team. We, as parents, are experienced climbers but we are still climbing alongside of our kids; we are still in danger of a fall. Whereas, parents that view themselves as coaches create an impression that they are beyond the climbing and now are demanding that their kids simply do what they say, not what they do. But that's just not the case; the Holy Spirit is shaping and changing us to be more like Christ (not Solomon) all the way to our graves. This means that we are climbing alongside and not standing on the sidelines barking out orders. Seeing your child as a less experienced equal is less adversarial and more focused on the journey together, and thus truer to the gospel. It helps you to major on empathy over accusation and ridicule. It gives you access to the grace you so readily accept from God on a daily basis. It gives you freedom from the frustration of living with a little sinner, as you see yourself as cut from the same cloth.

# I

# NATURAL PARENTING AND SPIRITUAL PARENTING

*"It is grace, not law, that teaches us."* Jerry Bridges, The *Disciplines of Grace*

WHEN MY WIFE, HAYLEY, AND I BROUGHT OUR DAUGHTER, ADDY, HOME FROM THE HOSPITAL we had absolutely no idea what we were doing. We went in as two and came out as three; it was as simple as that (if you don't mention the forty hours of labor and emergency surgery, but that's another story.) No pre-screening or training by some knowledgeable government employee or well-trained child-rearing expert was received; we were just sent out into the big dangerous world with a fresh human being in our hands and no clue what to do with her. As we struggled to figure out why she screamed, what she wanted, and why she wouldn't eat, one dark, warm night in August my physically and emotionally-drained wife looked at me through tear-filled eyes and said, "Can we take her back? Would they take her? I have no idea what I'm doing." The anguish was written all over her face. How come these things don't come with an owner's manual or at least some kind of instructional video?

It took us a few days, but eventually we started to get the hang of it. Maybe that's why they don't have mandatory nine-month courses on how to care for children because, ultimately, a lot of it just comes naturally to us: feed them, change them, answer their cries, keep them warm, protect them. We were made to do that, and while some might do it better than others, ultimately even the most uneducated of people raise children into adulthood, many times with great success. This natural inborn ability to care for our offspring is talked about in Matthew 7:9-10 where it spells out the natural bent to meet the needs of our kids this way, "which one of you, if his son asks him for bread, will give him a stone? Or if he asks for a fish, will give him a serpent?" The asking of this rhetorical question infers that we naturally meet our kids' needs rather than offer them stones and serpents (though some young boys may request them). This natural desire to do good for our kids isn't evidence of something spiritual but biological, of the natural parenting DNA that is in us all as we, by nature, attempt to do what is good for our children both physically and emotionally. This is spelled out in Paul's discussion of the morality of the unspiritual, "For when Gentiles, who do not have the law, by nature do what the law requires, they are a law to themselves, even though they do not have the law. They show that the work of the law is written on their hearts, while their conscience also bears witness, and their conflicting thoughts accuse or even excuse them" (Romans 2:14-15). In fact, except in the most heinous of hearts, there is the desire to do what we believe is best for our kids; it's just the going about it that is the challenge.

### Natural Parenting

Sometimes when we parent, it's hard not to let our own natural self-interest and self-protection take over. In some ways, parents and zookeepers have a few things in common. Zookeepers tend to the well being of the animals in their care, all the while being mindful of their own safety when they enter the cage. When the screaming starts and toys are thrown, we want to run towards that cage door to get out and let the next shift zookeeper take over ("Dad's home!") So, like a zookeeper, we serve our children all the while being mindful of our own safety and protection. We institute rules, insist on order, set boundaries, and do all we can to keep the animals safe and healthy, thus assuring the safety of our own hearts, bodies, and minds. Again, like the zookeeper, we carefully wield our power over creatures that could threaten us at any time while we attempt to domesticate them, teaching them to be good if they want their needs or wants met.

When you get to the bottom of it, natural parenting is about survival: survival of the child, the family, the community, and the species. The natural parent in us ultimately wants a better life for our kids than we had. If we were chameleons, we'd want our kids to have better camouflage then we had. If we were cheetahs, we'd want our cubs to be faster then us (eventually). Natural parenting is rooted in the hope and promise of evolution. We want them to evolve, to have more, do more, grow the family business, marry up, carry on our bloodline, and so we naturally do whatever it takes to assure our child is the fittest they can be so that they can survive and thrive.

For the natural parent, the law, regardless of how extensive, is an important tool in the safety and development of their children. Just like God gave the law to the young nation of Israel to protect and grow it in its infancy during barbaric times, so we give our infants and toddlers the law to hem them in and to protect them from touching a hot stove or running into the street. The law helps people to know the pitfalls of life and to avoid the dangers of our big bad world. So, the natural parent creates boundaries for their children, teaches them right from wrong, and ultimately, whether believer or not, shares with them the moral code that is itself defined by our righteous and moral God. Do not lie, do not steal, do not kill, honor your parents; these laws serve us well as a society and especially as parents.

I see the natural parent as serving the lifelong work of being a sort of building inspector, making sure things are up to code and issuing citations for non-compliance. This code is enforced by teaching them what is and isn't allowed, what is expected of them as contributing members of society, and what to do and not to do to be a "good child." As a result, the best-case scenario for natural parenting is the child makes progress in the improvement, evolution, and growth of their family tree. The worst-case scenario is being identified as unacceptable because of moral failure, and so being cut off, and, ultimately maybe even disowned.

### Spiritual Parenting

Natural parenting is a necessary aspect of child rearing; it's necessary for the survival of the species and its evolution towards a better way of life, as much now as it was when God first gave the law to Moses and the infant nation of Israel. Natural parenting is based on natural law, survival of the fittest, building civilization, and the desire for self-improvement. While everything that is natural was created by a supernatural God, for the New Testament believer, parenting doesn't stop with the natural but has to move deeper into the realm of the supernatural (or spiritual.) As believers we know that our children are spiritual beings and that our call is to not only teach them the law but to teach them that we are incapable of perfectly keeping that law. The entirety of the Old Testament teaches us just that and reveals to us the need for a Savior from our own lawlessness. A verse in the New

Testament sheds light on this idea with these words, "What, then, is the purpose of the laws given to Moses? They were added to identify what wrongdoing is. Moses' laws did this until the descendant to whom the promise was given came. It was put into effect through angels, using a mediator" (Galatians 3:19, GWT). So we see that we first needed the law so we could know what sin was (see Romans 3:20), but since the law could not save us, there needed to be a Savior who could. As we see in Galatians 3:24-27, "So then, the law was our guardian until Christ came, in order that we might be justified by faith. But now that faith has come, we are no longer under a guardian, for in Christ Jesus you are all sons of God, through faith. For as many of you as were baptized into Christ have put on Christ." This idea was further explained by Charles Spurgeon who once said, "The law is for the self-righteous, to humble their pride: the gospel is for the lost, to remove their despair."[ii]

**It is my contention then, that natural parenting is a necessary guardian of our children's lives only until they are able to see and grasp the gloriousness of God's grace.** Natural parenting should always be subservient and administered only through the filter of spiritual parenting. This should happen as soon as a child has ears to hear and eyes to see, even if we don't know if our child fully understands. Just as the law came first and showed us the sinfulness of our hearts, followed by grace and truth delivered through Christ, so then grace and truth has to become our response to the sinfulness of our children's hearts (see John 1:17). Spiritual parenting is based on this grace; a grace that none of us, adults or children alike, deserve, but are still generously given and, in turn, we must give to others including our little ones. This idea of giving grace because much grace has been given is seen in the parable that Jesus told about the man forgiven of his debt. In it we read:

*"Therefore the kingdom of heaven may be compared to a king who*

*wished to settle accounts with his servants. When he began to settle, one was brought to him who owed him ten thousand talents. And since he could not pay, his master ordered him to be sold, with his wife and children and all that he had, and payment to be made. So the servant fell on his knees, imploring him, 'Have patience with me, and I will pay you everything.' And out of pity for him, the master of that servant released him and forgave him the debt. But when that same servant went out, he found one of his fellow servants who owed him a hundred denarii, and seizing him, he began to choke him, saying, 'Pay what you owe.' So his fellow servant fell down and pleaded with him, 'Have patience with me, and I will pay you.' He refused and went and put him in prison until he should pay the debt. When his fellow servants saw what had taken place, they were greatly distressed, and they went and reported to their master all that had taken place. Then his master summoned him and said to him, 'You wicked servant! I forgave you all that debt because you pleaded with me. And should not you have had mercy on your fellow servant, as I had mercy on you?' And in anger his master delivered him to the jailers, until he should pay all his debt. So also my heavenly Father will do to every one of you, if you do not forgive your brother from your heart." (Matthew 18:23–35)*

This forgiveness for not being able to pay his own ransom and foot his own bill is the exact same story for us when it comes to the depth of the grace we as believers have received from God. For the forgiven sinner, grace is the most important thing in their life. It is the source of all hope, all faith, and all obedience. It is on this gift of grace that our spiritual lives are built because, without it, we would not have the redeeming work of Christ in our hearts. And without offering grace in abundance to our children, it's likely that they will not see God's grace for themselves through us, only in spite of us.

So natural parenting is based on the law while spiritual parenting, at its heart, is grace-centered and gospel-centered. It isn't dependent on performance or achievement but instead on the empathy of an old sinner walking alongside a young sinner that naturally, and through instruction, knows about the law and consequences but needs to be exposed to the supernatural knowledge of a grace that originates with the Father. Natural parenting is needed for the survival and health of the infant, toddler and child, but as soon as a child has ears to hear, as soon as a child has eyes to observe and absorb, the spiritual parent is walking and talking the things of God and not just the law that demands performance and justice, but, in far greater measure, speaking of the gospel of grace and Jesus' performance in our place.

A natural birth takes nine months, but a spiritual birth takes much longer and has no set gestation period. As a spiritual parent, the discomfort of pregnancy and anxiety for your child's spiritual birth can be exhausting and taxing in your own strength. It can be hard to labor years to see any spiritual fruit and many a parent will pray in anguish at their child's bedside wishing and hoping tomorrow would be the day that a visible spiritual birth would take place. But the blessed assurance we have in the gospel of grace is that we are not in control but God is. Our call is to trust him who is trustworthy and to faithfully walk alongside our child until that blessed day they testify to their own rebirth.

Without attention to spiritual parenting, you merely end up with a natural evolutionary process and neglect the spiritual life of both yourself and your child. As Christians, we must make the move from the natural to the supernatural, from the physical to the spiritual.

## Parenting is Discipleship

Let me be clear, this is not an issue of natural parenting versus spiritual parenting, of law versus grace. Both are a part of our lives of faith, but the law comes more naturally to us than grace. "Don't touch this, don't do that, mind your manners," is tangible, legible, enforceable, and it makes sense to even the unbelieving soul. Enforcing the law is our natural magnetic north (obeying it is another matter.) But **the call of a parent living in the Spirit is not to use the law to control or modify behavior but to reveal God's nature, our sinful nature, and our need for God's grace.** That's the real purpose of the law. The law is a precursor to grace and, thus, prepares us for our need for salvation as we see in Romans 7:7 "if it had not been for the law, I would not have known sin."

So I'm not suggesting abolishing the law and offering a hyper-permissive home of cheap grace to your children. What I am attempting to do is to explain the role of the parent as primary discipler to the child. For the spiritual parent, this is a move to a new covenant of parenting, even a new definition of the word "parenting"; that parenting *is* discipleship.

How we parent teaches our children what to value as they see and hear what we value. No matter how you are parenting now, no matter what spiritual emphasis you place on parenting, make no mistake, you are discipling your child. For better or for worse, your child is learning from you; they see what you value, dismiss, own, disown, and what you worship. They are being discipled by you in learning if their words and actions have to agree. They are learning from you if they can pick and choose their faith. And, ultimately, they are learning from you whether or not God is really in control. Yes, your child is being discipled, taught what to believe, whether you want to admit it or not. This is true with whomever your child spends the most time. Whether it be daycare workers, teachers, friends, relatives, or neighbor kids, they are all discipling your child on the nature of both God and man. This fact is sobering and unavoidable. The responsibility then is to choose those guiding influences wisely and to disciple your child through those significant relationships in their lives.

So the best spiritual parenting is one of intentional discipleship. Spiritual parenting doesn't eliminate or replace natural parenting, but frames the natural through the context and foreknowledge of the supernatural. It's really all about the priority of attention, attention to teaching them about the natural world through the lens of the supernatural. The spiritual parent bases every lesson and teachable moment on the foundational truths of who God is and who we are as distorted image bearers of God, saved by grace. Because we as parents have this foreknowledge of grace, the spiritual parent looks to transition as quickly as possible from natural parenting to spiritual parenting.

It has been my observation that most Christian parents stick to natural parenting (with an authoritarian foundation) throughout the teen years and only transition to spiritual parenting after the child leaves the nest. Let me just add here that I am able to write about this concept of spiritual parenting not because I've raised multiple children to adulthood but because of the hundreds of thousands of teens and young adults and their parents that I have spoken to and ministered to either in person or through the books that my wife and I have produced. Hearing from them and seeing the failure of natural parenting alone in their lives led us to raise our daughter differently. In our attempt to rebel-proof our home, we studied the reasons why children rebel and found that it is most often because there has been so little grace through spiritual parenting and far too much power and performance measured against the law through authoritarian methods.

This isn't a book about behavior modification or having a new kid by the end of the week. And it's definitely not about turning a sinner into a saint but, rather, about how sinners love one another and live with each other in the same kind of grace that God gives to all his children.

If you're still skeptical of my qualifications for writing a book on parenting, that's totally understandable. Certainly the experience of time and results can be an indicator of wisdom, but let me make one thing perfectly clear ~ the architecture of the house of grace stands on its own regardless of the outcome or output of my offspring because the blueprints are inked with the gospel.

**If we base fatherhood on the performance or outcome of the father's children, then God the Father must be a lousy one because just look at Adam (and me!)** Jesus called us to make disciples, not raise good, successful, and well-mannered children. This realization not only allows you to read a book on raising little sinners from someone like me, but it also releases you and me to raise children in a way where their performance can never injure or promote our own résumés. So we parent, not out of self-interest, but out of the realization that it is God who saves, by His grace, not the law or our own performance. This is true for us as parents and for our children alike.

So if safety, survival, and performance are the motivators for natural parenting, what motivates spiritual parenting? To answer that let's look at three spiritual reasons why families exist:

To grow the kingdom of God within the home.

To grow the kingdom of God outside the home.

To bring glory to God.

If you parent with any other aim or motivation, never moving past the natural, then it's, naturally, unspiritual. But you might say, "Michael, isn't spiritual discipleship the church's job? Aren't ministers more qualified?" No, discipleship is not solely the church's job; the parent should shoulder the lion's share of the load. I recently heard author Tim Kimmel say that the church should be like a Home Depot for discipleship with the church saying to the parent, "you can do it, we can help."

Parenting really is discipleship. That is the paradigm shift that's needed to begin this journey, sinners saved by grace discipling other sinners about this supernatural reality is the ground upon which you build a house of grace. Whether it is your family home, your church home, or your single-no-kids home where you host a bible study, we are all called to this process of spiritual parenting. We are all spiritual children that are created to be fruitful and multiply: all called to disciple and be discipled. So my hope for this book is not to make you a better parent but, instead, a more authentic minister of the gospel and a spiritual compass that constantly points to the all-Holy God of Grace for your children, neighbors, and co-workers.

So take a deep breath. We've laid the foundation that parenting is discipleship. Now we can start building your house of grace.

\* \* \*

## "Yes, grace but..." - Questions from a Reader

Q: *You said, "natural parenting is a necessary guardian of our children's lives only until they are able to see and grasp the gloriousness of God's grace." At what age are children spiritually aware enough for us to move past natural parenting?*

The most obvious answer is to look at the child's communication and comprehension development. Those two factors can help determine the spiritual content of our conversations. But I think a more important question than how soon, or at what age do we transition from natural to spiritual parenting, is this: is my natural parenting confirming the gospel of grace or contradicting the gospel of grace? When we, as parents, make natural parenting decisions on how to discipline our child, are we taking into account how that is going to re-enforce or contradict our future parenting decisions? So then, does the little smack, the raised voice, or the snapping tone lay a ground work for building a strong foundation of gospel parenting, or does it undermine or even build something, ultimately, unhelpful and ungospelish that we will have to tear down in the future?

As parents, we have no way of knowing for certain how much our infant, toddler or preschooler is absorbing, just because they don't articulate back to us what they are hearing, feeling and sensing. So that weighty unknown should be enough for us as parents, with a long view of discipleship, to treat our children with the grace that none of us deserve, even at ages contained by cribs and playpens. So let me answer the question "When should I start spiritual parenting?" with an old Indian proverb. Their answer to the question "when is the best time to plant a tree?" is "twenty years ago." "When is the second best time to plant a tree?" "Today." So it is the same with the question of when is the best time to start spiritually parenting my child.

Q: At what age can I start practicing a culture of grace and confession in my home?

By adopting the mindset of grace from birth, you create the muscle memory of confession and celebration in yourself and your child. Rather than saving it for a time when they fully understand, it is best to offer it as God does, freely and from birth. That means that we have to consider our babies to be sponges that are instantly soaking up either love and grace or discipline and demand. So when the newborn screams all night, grace. And when the toddler dumps their food on your clean floor, grace. The actions of grace are different for each age. The best way to offer grace is to remember that. You would never discipline a new born for spitting food on you, but you would for a ten-year-old. Every age has different needs for grace, and reminding ourselves of the developmental level of each particular child helps us to turn to grace over reprimand and discipline.

As far as confession is concerned, we always want to celebrate it. Especially when the child is young and just learning what the family stands for. If we want homes that are safe to confess in, we have to make confession an acceptable and healing norm.

When the parent's sin affects the child, or the child observes the parent's sin in relationship to herself, confession from a parent is like ipecac for the child's soul, getting them to expel something toxic soon after it was ingested after the parent unwittingly fed it to them. Confession from a parent to a child is really a practice of protecting your child from ingesting poison, the poison of observed unconfessed sin of the parent. It's proactive healing for the child and the parent (see James 5:16).

"Kids don't follow pretend experts on matters that concern them, they want to listen to people who get them, who are in the same pit they are in, and that's why being an authority on the abundant grace of God puts you squarely in their pit."

—House of Grace

# 2

# FOUR TYPES OF PARENTS

*"Some of the strongest appeals are made with mute lips, by godly fathers and saintly mothers who, around the fireside, feared God, loved his cause, and daily exhibited to their children and others about them, the beauties and excellencies of Christian life and conduct." E.M. Bounds*

WHEN I TOOK THE MYERS-BRIGGS PERSONALITY TEST, it only confirmed what I pretty much knew already. I am in ENTJ. That means that I'm an extroverted (though sometimes introverted,) intuitive, thinking, judge. I'm described as a field marshal by one test, and an otter yet in another. Do you know the tests I'm talking about? Have you taken one? They are great tools that are most often used to help perspective employers learn more about who you are without having to spend much time with you. They're good for awareness and placement and, if used properly, they are good for change as well. Most people, however, see their personality as such an integral part of who they are that they don't believe it can be changed, but that isn't wholly true. Personality tests can also help you to identify the parts of your personality that are inconsistent with the life of Christ ~ things like selfishness, worldliness and pride ~ and so, help you to spot those areas in your personality that you want to change. The idea that your personality is not a life sentence but an indicator of where you need more of him might seem unorthodox, but this idea is in keeping with the words of Ephesians 4:22-24, which say, "You were taught, with regard to your former way of life, to put off your old self, which is being corrupted by its deceitful desires; to be made new in the attitude of your minds; and to put on the new self, created to be like God in true righteousness and holiness" (Ephesians 4:22-24, NIV). Your personality isn't meant to be static, but forever changing under the pruning and perfecting of the Holy Spirit. In fact, knowing where you are now helps you better put on this new life.

So, while these personality tests come from the world of academia and business, many believers use them as diagnostic tools in the pursuit of faith. So it would stand to reason that like personality typing it would be helpful to look at research within academia regarding different parenting styles as well. One of the most interesting to me is an examination of four distinct styles of parenting.

During the early 1960s, psychologist Diana Baumrind studied over 100 small children and identified three styles that their parents commonly took in parenting them. She labeled these styles as authoritarian, authoritative, and permissive (or indulgent). In 1983, Eleanor Maccoby and John Martin[iii] added a fourth style: neglectful. While modern psychologists don't tend to look at life through the lens of faith, I believe there are some faithful insights into the choices we make in our parenting that we can glean from these studies in order to better understand who we are as Christian parents. Just like we can use personality tests to see the areas in our lives where we need redemption and change, so too we can use these parenting styles to help us better assess the faithfulness of our parenting. Just like personality tests, I suggest using what you read here as a guide to show you where you need improvement, rather than as a description of the tendencies you are stuck with. As believers, we are meant to be always changing, becoming more and more like our Savior, deepening our love for him as well as for his (and our) children. I urge you to be honest with yourself as you look at each of these four styles and also to be fearless as you see things in your past that may be less than faithful, and maybe even destructive. We cannot change unless we are willing to see who we really are and embrace who we know God wants us to be.

### Permissive and Indulgent

Growing up in Oregon, I spent a lot of time surrounded by hippie culture. My parents even owned two different Volkswagen microbuses. Even though we weren't a typical hippie family, there were plenty around us. You know the kind, they are always happy go lucky, laid back, nothing gets under their skin as they let their kids explore the world and define it for themselves. This kind of parent is often seen talking happily to a friend while junior climbs a lamppost stationed at the fence of the lion's den at the zoo. Permissive parents are just what the label suggests, permitting whatever will be. According to Baumrind, "the permissive parent attempts to behave in a non-punitive, acceptant and affirmative manner towards the child's impulses, desires, and actions." At its worst, the permissive parent allows the inmates to run the asylum. Because of that, they rarely discipline their children, after all discipline requires law and the permissive parent rejects the notion of excessive laws being healthy or even useful. But, as Baumrind says, "She [the parent] consults with him [the child] about policy decisions and gives explanations for family rules." This parenting democracy places value on the human mind to determine right from wrong and so allows both parent and child to make rules and decide on policies, if there even are any. In a Christian family this permissive style of discipline might take a slightly different shape as the parent uses the laws pertaining to proper behavior, such as sharing, using kind words, etc. But realizing that no one is perfect, the permissive parent quickly overlooks any failure in not keeping the law.

In a family that practices permissive parenting (with guiding suggestions, but not rules,) I have seen parents start out strong. "No shouting. Please use your inside voice." Then, "okay, keep it down." And finally, "All right, I'll do it, just stop shouting." Notice the progression, as the child misbehaves the parent starts out strong with a command, but as the misbehavior continues the permissive parent eventually gives into the force of the behavior and capitulates in order to get the ultimate behavior they wanted. This might seem like kindness or grace to the parent, but it is actually a mixed signal that ultimately teaches the child that brute force overpowers law and gets you what you want. Baumrind explains this kind of parenting when she says, "She (the parent) presents herself to the child as a resource for him to use as he wishes, not as an ideal for him to emulate, nor as an active agent responsible for shaping or altering his ongoing or future behavior. She allows the child to regulate his own activities as much as possible, avoids the exercise of control, and does not encourage him to obey externally defined standards. She attempts to use reason and manipulation, but not overt power to accomplish her ends." And while most permissive Christian families do tend to appreciate externally defined standards of the law, when they ultimately see the child as either too young to manage obedience or find it too destructive to insist on obedience, they easily sweep God's law under the rug in favor of silence, peace, or free will.

Researchers consider the permissive parent to be responsive but non-demanding. That means that the permissive parent tends to be nurturing and communicative. The best-friend parent fits this style. They are very involved, as a friend would be, but they don't make very many demands of their children. They respond to their child's needs pretty quickly, unless it's time to trust the child to figure it out on their own, in which case they lay back and trust God to lead them into the right choice, even if suffering may be the outcome.

On the positive side, children raised by this permissive parent tend to mature and find their independence quickly. As a best friend, you can find inroads into the life of your teenage or adult child, but you trade that for a lack of authority or control over their bad or dangerous choices.

But not all permissive parenting is a conscious choice; some of it's accidental. Parents who, either through choice or personality disorder, are self-obsessed, become more consumed with what happens in their own lives than their children's and so they often become permissive in an attempt to get the kids out of their hair and get onto more important things (like themselves.) This teeters close to neglectful parenting (which I will address in the next section). And while I completely understand the tendency to become fatigued by needy children and often want time to myself, I also see that at the root of this is a self-obsession that takes the focus not just off of my child, but also off of my God. I don't have time to go into the concept of dying to self right now (you could always get our book, *Die Young*,) but any study of the concept in scripture will quickly alert you to the fact that Jesus calls us to die to our self-serving ways. In fact, this study should lead you to the conclusion that selfishness is the exact opposite of love (more on this in Chapter Six -The Nine Marks of a Disciple pg.

151). No matter what your parenting style, if you think more of yourself than your kids then you are not truly loving your kids. Because the permissive parent allows their kids to experiment and to explore their world, as teens they are at nearly triple the risk of drug and alcohol use, according to studies.[iv]

Of course the opposite is also true. Obsessing over your kids, though it may feel like it, isn't loving them either. When we obsess over stuff our motive is self. How that obsessed-over thing or person makes us feel, what they give us, that all comes from a self-centered motivation. But love is never meant to be about self. In fact, it's the total opposite. Love denies self. And parents love properly when they consider their children to be the property of God, not of self. We don't own our children; we can't perfectly protect them or guard them against all danger. In the end, the only one who controls their destiny is their Father in Heaven. To think that we control it is to become obsessed with controlling our child. This obsession creates over-protective parents, helicopter parents, and fearful parents who guard their kids, believing that if a worst-case scenario happened to their child, it would destroy them. This parenting, in an attempt to keep God from allowing suffering, is not centered on the grace, kindness, and omniscience of God but on his wrath. It comes from a wrong view of who God is and who our kids are in light of who he is.

Depending on the personality of the child, this parenting style will either create a child that is spoiled rotten or spoiled sweet. But either way, these children most often never learn to control their own behavior or emotional life, and so selfishly learn to take whatever they want and are unequipped when they don't get what they want. The result, spiritually speaking, is a child who is unable to love anyone but themselves. When parents fail to teach children that love is an act of denying oneself in favor of another, they fail to teach them the single most important commandment ~ to love God and to love others.

In the latter part of the 1880s, a child was born without the ability to see or to hear. In order to please her, her parents gave her whatever she seemed to want. They thought this was how they could love her; after all it felt like love to them. But what it turned out to be was selfishness, as they did what made them feel best. They weren't trying to teach her how to love, how to show the fruit of the Spirit, but how to be happy. Her name was Helen Keller, and once Annie Sullivan taught Helen and her family how to love her by teaching her about her world, Helen went from holy terror to life long teacher, author, and speaker. If happiness is the goal of parenting, then we will have spoiled children who do not know the truth about love and therefore do not know the truth about Love Himself, God. Continually giving in to our child's passions isn't the kindness it feels like because it doesn't teach them love. It is not love for the permissive parent to give into all their children's whims simply to keep the peace, or to make the child (or themselves) happy.

As you can see there are a lot of spiritual drawbacks to this style of parenting. While the permissive parent responds quickly to the desires of their children, what the permissive parent often fails to do is to respond appropriately to the spiritual needs of their children, which often conflict with these desires. The indulgent parent tends to yield to the senses rather than the Spirit. This indulgence fails to teach the child about God and their own sinful nature. We need not confuse happiness with holiness. Giving your kids everything they want is not the way to love them.

The nature of God never changes, he is always the same and what he desires in our lives doesn't change with our mood or our exploration. When the indulgent parent fails to give the child any firm ground to stand on, it translates into a failure to disciple. As a discipler, you are an expert that the child calls on for guidance and counsel, unless your answer is always, "what do you think?" or "what does your heart tell you?" If you are going to establish yourself as an equal with no more or less knowledge than your child, you are not going to be seen as a counselor or a guide.

When a permissive parent lacks the ability to disciple their child in the way of faith, the default becomes situational ethics, if any ethics at all. You basically build your child into a ship without a rudder. Or, for the sake of this book's word picture, a mobile home on wheels, with no solid foundation.

## Neglectful

One of my daughter's favorite books and movies is *Matilda*, by Roald Dahl. In this classic work of children's fiction, Matilda's parents have a classic neglectful style. They treat her like a slave when they are with her, and leave her to her own devices while they are away, which is most of the time. One day her mother trots off to play cards all day and Matilda, a preschooler, wanders into town and discovers the library. The library becomes a sanctuary for her. She falls in love with reading and escapes her life by devouring all the books she can find. This idea is captivating to kids as they consider the possibility of independent living at such a young age, but no matter how interesting Matilda's life is, the life of a neglected child is anything but healthy and rewarding.

When a parent is disengaged they have no desire to make any demands on their child or to set any real limits on them because they just don't spend much time with them. Because of this empty relationship, when pressure *demands* they pay attention to their child, it is usually negative attention in the form of an angry outburst that is the end result. Neglectful parents are considered by psychologists to be low on both response and demand, sometimes only going so far as to meet basic needs, but always remaining detached.

Prioritization is the root of the problem. The neglectful parent has prioritized themselves over their kids and God. Whether it's because of financial or emotional stress, a lack of love in their own lives, or because of an addiction, the struggles of this world take priority over anything or anyone else. And the result of this kind of parenting, if you can call it that, is a child who learns early on that the parent's life is more important than theirs and, as a result, they will be found fending for themselves (like Matilda.) As quick as they are able, these kinds of kids make every effort to stop being dependent and seek to gain more autonomy and independence. As these kids grow, they become emotionally withdrawn in an attempt to keep themselves at arms length from the suffering of unrequited love. A study done by Maccoby and Martin (1983) analyzed adolescents, ages 14-18, and found that these children of neglectful parents scored the lowest in psychosocial development, school achievement, internalized distress, and behavior.

Spiritually speaking, like the permissive parent, the neglectful parent makes an idol of themselves and rejects the life of faith, whether they consciously know it or not. Neglect by a parent is abandonment. It teaches children that the very one given to protect and love them finds them unlovable. This then teaches the child that whoever the parent worships, or purports to worship, is a farce, whether it's themselves, or some other god. To attempt to call yourself and your children Christians while you worship at the altar of self is to most likely destine your children to a future that rejects all that your faith stands for.

There is no upside to neglect. There is no silver lining or hidden benefit for the child. Adult children of neglectful parents can spend the rest of their lives struggling against the pain inflicted by their neglect. If you were neglected as a child, I am truly sorry. Your parents sinned in relationship to you and that sin impacted your life deeply. Now, as a parent or future parent, you have the choice to follow in their footsteps, which I doubt you want to do, or to change your family tree. But certainly a feeling of ignorance might cloud your heart. You might feel like you have no role model for good parenting. And that would be true if you were not a believer, but as a believer you do have a role model: one whose perfect love is not only your salvation but also your inspiration. I pray that the pages of this book will help you to be inspired by his grace and to desire more of him that your children might know him more.

## Authoritarian

Recently, a production company emailed me about a reality TV show they were making. They wanted to know if I knew any family that would be willing to be followed around 24/7 by a camera crew so that the world could see how they live as a Christian household. What they were looking for was a family where purity, in the form of isolating their kids from the world, was practiced. What they didn't say, but I know from the nature of reality TV, was they wanted a family that they could make fun of, that might implode before the viewing audience or, at the very least, could be mocked for their rigid ways. In a nutshell, they wanted an authoritarian family to sensationalize.

The non-believing world expects strong Christian families to lean towards this authoritarian style. Being lovers of the law, they expect Christians to demand a strict adherence to not only God's law but to the laws of etiquette and other man-made rules. This is not, however, a strictly Christian parenting style, though it does tend to be motivated by religious values. The authoritarian parent is identified in Baumrind's study as demanding but not responsive. "The authoritarian parent attempts to shape, control, and evaluate the behavior and attitudes of the child in accordance with a set standard of conduct," says Baumrind, "usually an absolute standard, theologically motivated and formulated by a higher authority." On the surface this might appeal to most of my readers, since we, as Christians, know the importance of God's law and the requirements on us as parents to teach it to our children (see Deuteronomy 6). Baumrind goes on to say that the authoritarian parent "values obedience as a virtue and favors punitive, forceful measures to curb self-will at points where the child's actions or beliefs conflict with what she thinks is right conduct. She believes in keeping the child in his place, in restricting his autonomy, and in assigning household responsibilities in order to inculcate respect for work." So, the authoritarian essentially believes that they have to enforce the law and punish failure to obey in order to protect their kids from themselves. That's why reality TV brings in the big bucks, because the more diligently mommy and daddy try to "protect" their kids by controlling them, the more drama is created.

The study goes on to say that authoritarian parents do not "encourage verbal give and take, but they believe that the child should accept their word for what is right." Because of the requirements on strict obedience, the authoritarian values the use of "punitive and forceful measures to curb self-will," as Baumrind further points out. These punitive and forceful measures, also known as punishment, go hand in hand with the law, especially when the law is meant to save. Parents who look at the law as their child's salvation, be it saving them from hell or saving them from improper conduct, believe that failure to obey the law must end in punishment. A parent without the power to punish loses the ability to make the demands. Law without punishment is toothless.

In my estimation, in this approach, the parent unwittingly must assign to themselves the attributes of infallibility and perfection because this is the position one must take in order to insist that, "everything I say is right and you cannot argue with me or there will be punishment." This authority has to be established in order to demand total obedience and to sustain order. If the parent should be seen as fallible and sinful then they would lose the control they rely on in order to demand their children live how they say.

Relying on their role as law giver and enforcer, authoritarians often find themselves saying things like, "because I said so," "don't talk back," "do as I say, not as I do", "don't disobey me," or "you WILL respect me!" The authoritarian puts the focus on the performance level of their child's work or activity and so they act as judge, jury, and executioner on that performance. The parent executes judgment on all of their actions because, at the heart of it, they either want to teach their children strict obedience or simply improve their own living conditions.

I know a family that lived this way. In order to teach obedience to the kids, the parents would have them line up at the end of the day and list all the stuff they had done wrong since they got up. Of course, as judge and jury the parents would then pass their sentence and give them their due punishment. What they were trying to do was teach their kids the depth of their sinfulness and of God's goodness that can't stand their 'badness'. The outcome was well-behaved, submissive little kids who quickly did what they were told and generally stayed out of the parents way. This ends badly in two ways: either they rebel and run wild once they are no longer under the power of the parent or, worse, they become legalistic and see their keeping of the law as the thing that saves them (see the elder brother in the parable of the prodigal.)

Once a parent determines they are judge and jury, they tend to elevate family laws that their children must follow to the level of God's law. It is here that the parent adds to biblical law the laws of proper social behavior, such as keeping elbows off of the table, taking shoes off in the house, along with laws that simply make life easier on the parent.

My wife and I have chosen to homeschool our daughter for the time being. As homeschoolers, we are thrown into several stereotypes regarding our lifestyle. The biggest and most often voiced is, "don't they miss out on the social?" Usually what people mean by that is they have seen so many homeschooling families who have children who are socially inept, that the critics end up assuming the culprit is homeschooling itself. Yet, our daughter and many of her homeschool friends are not only social butterflies, but can hold meaningful conversations with adults and peers alike. And Baumrind's research gives us a clue as to why many homeschoolers fall into the socially stunted trap. According to her study, social incompetence is the result of the authoritarian parenting tendencies of many homeschooling families. Her study found that children raised by authoritarians actually do "have less social competence because the parent generally tells the child what to do instead of allowing the child to choose by him or herself." The result of this model ~ of telling the child what to do instead of allowing them to choose for themselves ~ is that it creates a mindless child. They are mindless because they have no need to think for themselves when their parents do it for them. In this type of family, the kids go into a kind of "autopilot" where they do what they have to do and no more, because more could lead to punishment. Social skills are learned, not by obediently following the rules but by learning to discern the Spirit and what he would have you do in relationship to others. We are to serve others for the glory of God.

Social skills are important in the life of faith because without them we are unable to carry out the Word of God in the world around us. And even beyond that, when kids are not taught to think on their own they lack the spiritual gift of discernment as they have spent their lives being spoon fed the law of God rather than ingesting it for themselves and making a hearty meal of it. Having never been taught to reason and to seek God on their own they look to the law to save them, as it is the only thing that has saved them in the past. But, the law was never meant to save but to show us the sin in our lives that we might realize our need for a Savior (see Galatians 3:21-22).

And studies back this up. One particular study says that strict parenting more than doubles the teen's risk for heavy drinking.' Unfortunately, because of their lack of discernment and skill when it comes to social situations, drinking gives them the sensation of social ease. This is why once this child is out on their own all bets are off as they run away, arms waving, in the direction of all that their parents forbade when they were in control. Of course, this can easily turn into anti-social behavior, but more frequently ends in a strained relationship between teen and parent and later adult-child and parent.

The cultures that have this style of parenting most deeply rooted in their societies are Asian and Muslim cultures where their religious beliefs and social mores center on honor and shame. They tend not to embrace grace and aren't necessarily out to disciple their children in faith in Christ and salvation by grace alone. However, Baumrind's study also suggests that deeply religious Christian families in the U.S. tend to gravitate to the authoritarian style.

Some authoritarian parents might believe that you can never have too many rules, but most of us never notice our own laws creeping into our families. But the truth is that most of the law that we enforce in the lives of our children has nothing to do with faith and everything to do with convenience, control, order, and appearance. We create these laws to assure the successful functioning of our family unit and to ensure that our kids will be law abiding and contributing members of society, but that's not the goal of the discipling parent. The success of your child in the areas of tidiness, science, math, or even etiquette is not the defining element of her life.

Her life is defined by who she worships. An emphasis on the demands of success and social graces create a gospel of works and these works will neither save your child nor the world around them, but instead sentences them to a life of idolatry as they learn to serve something other than the Creator.

Discipleship is not based on presenting the law and then policing it. In fact, no one will ever be saved by strict obedience to the law (see Romans 3:20). So, why would we attempt to teach it as salvation? But that's just what we unwittingly do when make obedience to the law the salvation for our kids; when, in order to be saved from punishment, harshness, frustration or anger, they have to do what we want done when we want it done. Now, some might say, "I know that strict obedience won't save my kids, but I'm just training them up so they can avoid sin now and in the future." Once again, this approach creates a culture that values sin avoidance and inevitably cultivates sin concealment. And that, in turn, discourages confession and withholds training for sin rebound and healing for and from one another.

The law was never meant to save us, but to point to the holiness of God, the sinfulness of man, and our need of a savior. And so, in order to raise a child in Christ and through Christ, we have to share with them the grace that God so freely gives to us. If we never travel past Malachi, the last book in the Old Testament, then we will never make it to the cross. In order to offer the gospel to our kids, we've got to bring them to the cross.

### Authoritative

In the Victorian era of the early 1900s, authoritarian parenting was in vogue. Children were meant to be seen and not heard. They were expected to live like little adults and obey the real adults. In the 1960s, with studies like those done by Baumrind, parents began to look at parenting in a different light. And so the authoritative parenting style began to appeal more to modern man than the former, stricter parenting norm.

According to her study, "Authoritative parenting is characterized by a child-centered approach that holds high expectations of maturity." This child-centered focus of the authoritative style can have many Christian parents cringing. Making the child the center of your world sounds indulgent and dangerous. And obviously it can easily devolve into permissive parenting where the child becomes the obsession of the family. But let's dive in deeper to her description of authoritative parents. "Authoritative parents can understand how their children are feeling and teach them how to regulate feelings. They often help their children to find appropriate outlets to solve problems. Authoritative parents encourage children to be independent but still place controls and limits on their actions. Extensive verbal give-and-take is not refused, and parents try to be warm and nurturing toward the child." We can't argue that helping our kids to learn to regulate their feelings is a biblical value. After all, God's word is filled with commands on learning to deny ourselves, to resist temptation, and not surrender to the desires of the flesh. So this idea should make sense to the Christian parent's mind. And the need for a guide in the area of feelings and actions, can explain the need for some kind of verbal give-and-take. This idea might better explain a more "child-centered" house. Shutting down their feelings, as the authoritarian style is prone to do, doesn't allow for understanding and discernment in the child's mind, only blind obedience. So, in order to help the child through difficult emotional issues, we will often find ourselves having to forcibly divert from our plans to focus on the child. As believers, we are called by God's Word to show kindness, mercy, patience and love, yes even to people who are under eighteen, and so this approach of interacting in a warm and nurturing way toward the child is consistent with our faith.

Baumrind's explanation of punishment in the authoritative style is obviously less strict. She notes that, "authoritative parents set limits and demand maturity, but when punishing a child, the parent will explain his or her motive for their punishment. Children are more likely to respond to authoritative parenting punishment because it is reasonable and fair. A child knows why they are being punished because an authoritative parent makes the reasons known. They are attentive to their children's needs and concerns, and will typically forgive and teach instead of punishing if a child falls short."

Because of the high parental responsiveness and demand, these children are less likely to rebel. Studies confirm show that kids raised by authoritative parents are the least prone to heavy drinking[vi]. That is in part, due to the fact that the ultimate goal of the authoritative parent is to nurture socially responsible and cooperative children who are able to self-regulate.

Baumrind and other psychologists consider authoritative parenting to be a healthy balance between permissive and authoritarian. That is to say, that they are a healthy balance of both demand and response. Many well-meaning Christians would say the same thing, clearly identifying authoritative as a good balance between law and grace with appropriate discipline that's not heavy handed but suitable for the age and maturity of the child. This approach and view of authoritative parenting is all about balance. For most, it is the lesser of four evils; it's the best a psychologist can do that we can squeeze into our biblical worldview.

But this idea of balance is a deceptive one. It sounds right and good, fair and even-handed, but in fact, balance is inconsistent with grace. That's because balance refers to measuring out two things so they are equal in weight; meaning that for every grace given there must be an equal amount of punishment, otherwise the scales would become unbalanced and the parent would slip into the less desirable 'permissive' descriptor. So, in an attempt to remain 'balanced' many parents measure the amount of grace they give, they 'pick their battles,' punishing some confession while appreciating others, and they reserve grace for special occasions.

While the idea of balance might sound good to our ears, what it creates is unpredictability for the child: "will they punish me today or give me grace?" It all depends on the record books; where do they stand on their grace limit? As long as our measure of how much grace we give our kids is limited by the amount already given or is reserved for only special occasions, we will continue to view and communicate that grace is optional. And if grace is optional then what does that say about grace? That it is given on the basis of merit or, worse, whim? When this happens grace becomes just another weapon in the war on sin, wielded alongside of the law rather than taking its place. It's then when we sorely misunderstand grace. In turn, we misrepresent grace as not so amazing and certainly not so extravagant.

For the spiritual parent, this apparently sensible and balanced approach appears to be the best we can do. And so, raising socially responsible and cooperative children who are able to self-regulate becomes the goal, and if you can't be a true expert on all this goodness then you can at the very least resort to, "don't do as I do, do as I say." The trouble with this logic is that **kids don't follow pretend experts on matters that concern them, they want to listen to people who get them, who are in the same pit they are in, and that's why being an authority on the abundant grace of God puts you squarely in their pit.** A simple shift in perspective like this changes your function in parenting from being a performance coach to being a discipler.

What I would like to do from this moment in the book forward is redeem and redefine the authoritative style to mean this: an authoritative parent is one that is an authority on being a sinner who could never keep the law, who was saved by grace and serves a holy

God. From this perspective, authoritative parenting can never be confused with any other parenting style. Firstly, they are nothing like the permissive parent who rejects the idea that the law is good for anything, or at the very least makes the law less important than grace. On the contrary, the authoritative parent understands that the most amazing thing about grace is that the law exists. If the law didn't exist, grace would have no foil. Offering abundant and amazing grace to your child can't be confused with permissive parenting, because the permissive parent has no law to make the grace amazing.

Secondly, the authoritative parent is nothing like the authoritarian parent who finds grace too dangerous to offer their kids. On the contrary, the authoritative parent devotes themself to teaching their kids the single most important thing in the history of the world, God's amazing grace, and they do it not by talking about it, but by offering it, by mimicking it's giver; Jesus Christ. And they know that in order to understand the depth of grace they have to understand not only their need for it, but the free availability of it.

In order for authoritative parenting to be a balance of the other styles it must embrace those other styles equally, but I suggest that it does nothing of the sort. The gospel-centered authoritative parent's goal is not behavior modification or performance, but revealing the very heart of God to their children, embracing his law as essential only in so much as it reveals the nature of God himself, our sinfulness to ourselves, and our desperate need for a Savior. In short, the authoritarian is an authority over the child, while the authoritative parent, from the heart level to the functional definition, must be an authority *on life* for the child: more specifically, an authority on living life as a sinner saved by the grace of a holy God.

\* \* \*

### "Yes, grace but..." - Questions from a Reader

*Q: Are you saying that obedience isn't an important lesson? Ephesians 6:1 says, "Children obey your parents in the Lord." How do we teach this to our kids if we aren't telling them to obey us?*

Why is obedience an important lesson? Perfect obedience is impossible; there's a lesson! OK, I'm being a little bit playful here. Try teaching that obeying your parents is a good thing *for them*. Talk to your kids about the natural consequences of not obeying a parent; getting hurt, lost, sick, arrested, and not enough rest all come to mind. "Because I'm the boss" or "because the Bible says so" offers no incentive and it's likely they haven't owned their faith yet (more on that in Chapter 7.) Training someone or something to obey is relatively easy while you wield enough power and exert enough control. The trick is to become an authority in your child's life that is an advocate for them and can be trusted (more on that in Chapter 6!) Ask yourself, "Am I easy to obey? Am I harsh and demanding? Do I say 'Yes' more than 'No'?" I find that parents that find ways to say "Yes" to their children more often than "No" tend to have children that obey because they know from muscle memory that a "Yes" is right around the corner. It's also important to remember that obedience can be trained through cheerleading right behavior just as much as rebuking bad.

*Q: How do we teach our kids to honor their parents in grace? Aren't they required to honor us, and doesn't that mean we have to enforce their honor?*

This question sounds a lot like the last one but it's actually different because obeying your parents and honoring your parents are two different things. So, let me answer this question with another question: "Does God force us to honor him?" Should we honor him? Absolutely! But does he force us to? What if he did? How would you feel about someone so much more infinitely powerful than you making sure you honor him or else? It's a shocking thought, I know. Here's how you teach your kids to honor you:

You let them see and hear you honoring *your* parents.

You pray and strive to be easier to honor.

One of the most powerful realities about honor is demonstrated in the fact that the Medal of Honor is not given to the highest-ranking soldier but, instead, only to those that are so obviously deserving of honor because of their humble sacrifice and faithfulness.

"The purpose of parenting is discipleship because **parenting is discipleship**. Discipleship in the church for adults is really just a form of re-parenting; teaching people who God is and who they are with and without him because they didn't effectively learn this in their own home or they need it supplemented."

— House of Grace

# 3

# THE PURPOSE OF PARENTING

*"Discipleship must be based on God's grace."* - Jerry Bridges, *The Discipline of Grace*

I WROTE MY FIRST BOOK IN 2005 and, since that time, I've published almost forty books along with my wife, Hayley. Around two-thirds of those books are for teens and young adults and the rest are for what I like to call "former teens;" I've been using that phrase for over ten years. It didn't dawn on me until I was writing this book that this turn of phrase was the beginning of the philosophy that became *House of Grace*. I started using 'former teens' in place of 'adults' to get parents and influencers to remember what it was like being a teen. Not to wistfully wish to go back in time, but to have adults extend more empathy and understanding for their kids in the teen years.

After forty books in ten years, you would think I would have found my purpose in writing; that thing that everyone searches for that explains why we're here; that energizes us and makes us feel most alive, but you would be wrong. My purpose, the time when I feel most alive and my brain is firing on all cylinders, is when I'm speaking to groups about God and life. It may be a sermon preached at a church, dinner conversation with a group of friends, or a weekend conference for teens and their parents. Regardless of the setting and my preplanned notes, I love when the Spirit moves and something comes out of my brain (and mouth) at the last minute that I wasn't expecting and I see light bulbs go on in the audience. Those moments are sacred to me. When I come up with something that is too good to be true and can't be attributed to my hard work and study, but are just simply true, I feel God working through me and in spite of me. This happened recently when I was speaking at a church for a four-week series on how to build a house of grace. The night before I was to teach for the second time, I was sitting in a hotel restaurant trying to fix a problem I had with my talk. I ended up doodling on my napkin something random similar to the image below.

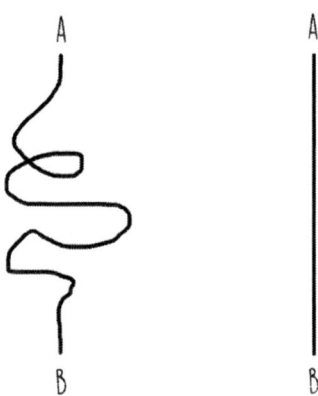

It was two lines or paths, side by side, both starting at point A and both ending up at point B. On the left is a squiggly meandering line, probably twice the distance in length to the line on the right, which was a straight direct path from point A to B. That little napkin was a gift from God, a love note I inserted into my talk at the eleventh hour. The next day at the church, I illustrated the two lines and asked these questions (and ask them of yourself as you read. If point A is watching TV and point B is my daughter brushing her teeth before bed or if point A is your house and point B is dropping off your child at school:

- Which of these paths is good and which is bad?
- Objectively, what's good about the squiggly indirect path?
- What's bad about the indirect path?
- What's good about the direct path?
- Is there anything bad about the direct path?
- Lastly, in your role as parent, what is the goal?

**What is the purpose of parenting?** This was that light bulb moment on the napkin and in the crowd that next day in the church: the purpose of parenting is not getting to 'B' the fastest and most efficient way possible. The purpose of parenting is also not accumulating as many Bs as possible in a day or over the course of the first eighteen years of our child's life. **The purpose of parenting is discipleship, and discipleship can happen along the straight path or the twisty path.** Some (like me) would argue that the twisty path provides more opportunity for discipleship than the straight path!

We, as parents, tend to forget what the journey of childhood through the teen years was like; we're bored (or jaded) with the simplicity and wonder of youth and scoff at the lack of responsibilities or at least how overwhelming life can feel to kids and teens. So when we're trying to get Junior or Princess to school on time and they stop dead in their tracks with wonder to stare at an ant carrying something ten times its size, we almost yank their arms out of their sockets because "we've gotta go" because we stopped 'wondering' at ants a long time ago. Again, it's easy for us to lose empathy for our kids because we just don't remember. So when our daughter freaks out because her "bestie" posted a picture of her online that made her look fat or our son silently stews about being made fun of for his voice cracking in class, it can be hard to relate and easy to tell them to get over it and it's no big deal. But it is a big deal to feel all alone and like no one understands. But God didn't (and doesn't) keep his holiness, wisdom, and love at a distance. He sent his son to live a life out among us to empathize with us and disciple us. Try remembering this visual when considering empathy. You know the best Christmas present ever for a two year old? The big cardboard box. How long have you been alive? Two, three, four decades? More? Cardboard boxes have lost their wonder to you. You've seen everything that can be seen, but your kid stops dead in their tracks when they see a commercial for a new toy or a cloud that looks like SpongeBob. As parents obsessed with point B, it's easy to rob our children of their wonder because we simply miss the purpose of parenting.

**The purpose of parenting is discipleship because parenting is discipleship.** Discipleship in the church for adults is really just a form of re-parenting; teaching people who God is and who they are with and without him because they didn't effectively learn this in their own home or they need it supplemented. We are constantly discipling whether we realize it or not; we are teaching our kids what we worship and who we worship. We are teaching them what to value and where our salvation lies. This fact was so important that it was the last thing Jesus said while here on earth, "Go therefore and make disciples of all nations, baptizing them in the name of the Father and of the Son and of the Holy Spirit, teaching them to observe all that I have commanded you. And behold, I am with you always, to the end of the age" (Matthew 28:19-20). Notice that Jesus did not command us to discipline all the nations, that's because good discipline is a by-product of discipleship. The law of discipline begs something to be done while the grace of discipleship reminds us of what has *already* been done. When we teach our kids the grace of discipleship over the law of discipline, we don't leave off teaching them God's law and what pleases him, we just do it in light of his amazing grace and Great Commission. In other words, we offer them the law as something that points to the perfection and righteousness of God, as we see in Psalm 19:

*"The law of the Lord is perfect, reviving the soul; the testimony of the Lord is sure, making wise the simple; the precepts of the Lord are right, rejoicing the heart; the commandment of the Lord is pure, enlightening the eyes; the fear of the Lord is clean, enduring forever; the rules of the Lord are true, and righteous altogether. More to be desired are they than gold, even much fine gold; sweeter also than honey and drippings of the honeycomb."* (Psalm 19:7-10)

This same law described as the answer to our souls' longings and our hearts' complaints is mirrored in Philippians 4:8 where we are told to think about "whatever is true, whatever is honorable, whatever is just, whatever is pure, whatever is lovely, whatever is commendable, if there is any excellence, if there is anything worthy of praise, think about these things." So, in both Psalm 19 and Philippians 4, as we ponder the precepts of God and think on them, we are given the peace of God. But how many kids in the world do you imagine see the law as such a wonderful and amazing thing? More readily they, like our daughter's friend, when told by Addy that God didn't want us to be unkind to our siblings, said, "God says this, God says that, blah, blah, blah!" This is the result of a child that is tired of hearing about God's law because all it does is constrain her actions, tells her what to do, and most likely results in her punishment when she doesn't obey.

For a lot of us, parenting is one of a million things that we have to do in a single day and the most urgent needs tend to get the most urgent attention. When that happens the quiet and patient call of discipleship gets sacrificed for the urgent. As Sunday rolls around, parents then breathe a sigh of relief as they send their kids off for an hour of godly wisdom and teaching and goldfish crackers, thanking the Lord that there is someone whose job it is to treat their kid's spiritual life as the most urgent task on their list. But the unfortunate result of our harried lives is that discipleship happens for only one hour out of the 168 hours a week that we are directly responsible for our kids. That means spiritual discipleship (happening solely through the church) amounts to 1/168th of a child's life.

*Allow that to sink in a minute.* The school system has our kids 16% of the time, the church has them one half of 1% of the time, and we possess control over the remaining 83% of their schedule (really 100% of it.) And, if you agree that discipleship happens shoulder-to-shoulder (regardless of the spiritual intent), then this ratio should be eye-opening because you and I, as parents, have the lion's share of shoulder time.

It can be easy to compartmentalize the spiritual growth of our children into the 1% of Sunday mornings and Wednesday nights, but if discipleship is happening all of the time, then why aren't we parenting/discipling the remaining 83% of our children's lives with discipleship in mind? Why isn't discipleship (parenting and reparenting) the subject of conversation in churches? Knowing that some 75% of kids raised in church-going homes will stop attending church by the time they reach their early twenties, many church leaders have created elaborate plans to do something about it. From changing the church building to changing traditions, music, dress codes, and even attitudes, they've worked hard at making church more palatable to a younger generation. While I admire their heart and spirit, I question their approach. I don't believe that the problem requires so much global change. Certainly a lot of those cultural trappings of the church may be outdated for communicating the gospel in the 21st century, but they aren't the problem, only the by-product. The root of millennial rebellion to the paternal church started when the church and the parents in it agreed that discipline was the parent's job and discipleship was the church's job, functionally separating the two and handicapping both in the process.

There is a cultural norm within the church where we quickly believe that if something sounds beneficial to us, it must be biblical. Like the saying "cleanliness is next to godliness;" it's beneficial but it's not in the Bible. And nowhere is non-biblical moral reasoning more attached to the gospel than in our churches children's ministries. If you have spent any time at all in church, then you have heard it said that parents must learn to discipline their children. In order to be good and productive members of society (a humanistic goal,) whether it be in our country or in the church, parenting requires discipline. That's why it shouldn't have surprised me as I watched my seven year-old daughter's church musical and heard the narrator say, "God loves you most when you obey your parents." This statement flew under the radar of the well-meaning curriculum writers, church staff and volunteers because it sounds like such a helpful thing (at least for the parents). This easily can become the subtext of discipline in the family, "Obey and you will be a good child and we will love you." But this logic has a fatal ungospelish flaw to it that I hope I don't have to point out but will, just to be safe: teaching our kids that keeping the law is what makes them good and acceptable and loved (most loved!) is unbiblical to the core and firmly rejects the gospel which says, it is by grace you have been saved, not by works so that no one can boast (see Ephesians 2:8).

Fortunately, following the law will never be the reason for our acceptance. Unfortunately, many well-intentioned teachers have instructed parents the exact opposite by telling them that teaching the law to our kids is as simple as teaching them that they must honor us because we are their parents and they must show us the respect we deserve. The law then becomes a necessity in the life of the child, something they must, above all else, fulfill for their parents. But the reason Christ came was because man was unable to keep the law. So why would any gospel-believing parent insist that their kids do the very thing that Christ's crucifixion proves they can't? After all we read in Galatians 2:21 "for if righteousness were through the law, then Christ died for no purpose." That means that your kids cannot get their lives right through being good kids, through honoring you, or through learning to respect their elders, and any attempt to build on this foundation will only create moralistic adults who put more stock in their own abilities and failures than in the grace of God. When my wife, Hayley, was young she was spanked only once. She was almost always obedient, doing whatever her parents asked, but it wasn't because they enforced the law with punishment for any failure to comply. On the contrary, it was because of her deep love for her parents. She often tells the story of how much she loved and even idolized her father. Though he didn't know the gospel at the time, he exemplified the grace of God to her in her early childhood years. Like many little girls, she saw him as perfect, the strongest man in the world, who could do everything she couldn't, and she adored him. Because of that she wanted to do all she could to please him. Out of that desire came an obedience that wasn't born out of fear or self-protection but out of love and adoration. In this simple example of a child's love for her parent we can see the image of our love for God as seen in 1 John 4:18-19:

"There is no fear in love, but perfect love casts out fear. For fear has to do with punishment, and whoever fears has not been perfected in love. We love because he first loved us."

This is one of the greatest verses in the Bible on parenting, discipline, and discipleship. Yet, we never use it that way. This passage teaches us that the very nature of God is love, and so as we abide in him we too abide in love. As we abide, we find that there is no fear in us that expectantly waits for punishment. His perfect love and grace gets rid of all the fear of punishment for disobedience, and instead allows us to obey out of love, not a love that we generate, but one that comes because he first loved us.

The early church fathers asked the question, "What is the purpose of man?" And the answer they came up with has been repeated for centuries by theologians, families, and even children the world over: the purpose of man is to glorify God (see Isaiah 43:7). That means that no matter what we do, in everything from washing the dishes, to driving to work, to teaching our kids, we exist to glorify God. And we most glorify God when we reveal the depths of his love for us to those around us. As the primary source of our children's spiritual direction, it would then stand to reason that the purpose of parenting, for the Christian, is to disciple our kids in the love of God. If the love of God drives out fear because fear has to do with punishment, then discipling our kids in the love of God would mean that the fear of punishment is inconsistent with parenting.

Unfortunately, most of us have mistakenly replaced the word 'punishment' within our families with 'discipline' thinking them to be interchangeable. But I do not believe that they are. To make sure we are on the same page, let me state that punishment is when a parent takes a punitive action against a child for breaking a rule with the purpose of inflicting emotional and/or physical pain in order to dissuade similar actions in the future, as well as to pay some kind of debt or penalty for the transgression. Discipline, on the other hand is not just a nicer version of punishment. By way of example, let's take a look at 2 Timothy 1:7, *"For the Spirit God gave us does not make us timid, but gives us power, love and self-discipline"* (NIV). Now, to see if the words are interchangeable, replace 'self-discipline' with 'self-punishment' and read the verse again. Does the meaning change? Yes, that's because we inherently know that there is nothing punitive about discipline in the context of discipleship. But to discipline a child with a discipleship focus, I have found that it is far kinder to apply discipline (the noun) instead of discipline (the verb.) Dallas Willard defined discipline (the noun) this way: "A discipline is an activity within our power—something we can do—which brings us to a point where we can do what we at present cannot do by direct effort.[vii]" The gospel of grace, it would seem, when applied to parenting would suggest that we are to develop *disciplines* in our child's life through shoulder-to-shoulder discipleship, not to *discipline* our children into good behavior through nose-to-nose punishment. We inherently know this when thinking about church life. We would all agree that no one punishes someone into a life of faith; that would be a very ugly church to attend! But we win people with love and genuine soul concern for the person being discipled.

The last sentence in the passage in 1 John teaches us that the source of our love is his love. This truth is foundational to our faith and should be to our parenting as well. We have to understand that we love not because we've been taught the law and told what is right and wrong, but because we are loved. It is out of his abiding love for us that we then learn to love him and his law. As we read in 1 John 5:3, "For this is the love of God, that we keep his commandments. And his commandments are not burdensome." It is out of our love for God that we learn to love his commandments and refuse to say, "God says this, God says that, blah, blah, blah." Because we love him out of his initiated love, his law delights us as it points to his holiness.

So many times as parents we mistakenly believe that obedience is achieved through a thorough understanding of the law and the promised punishment for any failure to keep it. We look at punishment as an essential tool for teaching our children about their faith, for protecting them from sin, and for keeping them on the narrow road. But when punishment is placed on us from an external force, its focus is physical over spiritual, self over soul. On the contrary, spiritual discipline is internal, and is not a state of responding to an outside force, but a state of being.

Spiritual discipline isn't something that we can punish into the lives of our kids; it is something that we must disciple into their lives. When a parent takes the time to disciple their child, they will eventually find that they have little need to punish them. That is because discipleship teaches children how to respond to the promptings of the Spirit. Not that they always get it right, but spiritual discipline gets its fuel from God not from man as is seen in the fruit of the Spirit that is explained in Galatians 5:22-23. The self-control (self-discipline) that the Spirit provides us is far superior to any external demands a parent could put on their child.

Every so often, our daughter struggles with procrastination at bedtime. My wife or I will give her an instruction to brush her teeth or go select a bedtime book and she will delay to the point that she will lose the privilege of book reading for the night. When she does lose book time, she's very upset. And in the past, I would remind her that there are consequences for her (in)actions. But when grace and discipleship became our foundation for parenting, I turned nose-to-nose into shoulder-to-shoulder and began to say things like, "I know you miss your book time. You can't let a lack of self-control determine your destiny and to choose for you, because your flesh will always choose wrong and leave you disappointed." After that explanation I'd stay in her room longer than usual. And then the next night, I'd continue discipling her by saying before bed, "Now don't let a lack of self control decide what you miss out on tonight." So the discipline that she received was not punishment, but rather the fruit of my self-discipline in walking her through the fruit of the Spirit versus the fruit of the flesh (more on this later.) And so when a child is being discipled, self-discipline is nurtured from an early age. When that happens, it allows the parent to operate more freely in the way of grace-giver over law-keeper, of life-guide over wronged-royal.

We know a little girl who is diligently discipled by her parents and is very aware of their habits of kindness and grace toward her. Because of this, she was quickly led to tears as she found herself acting selfishly towards her mother. Because she had been raised to recognize and experience the fruit of the Spirit, and to be sensitive to the conviction of the Holy Spirit, when she woke up her mother in the middle of the night, she immediately confessed her selfishness. Discipline wasn't necessary because she had already confessed her error; she was offered comfort and healing instead. Conviction did the work of discipline, but only because of her love for her mother that grew out of her mother's love that was there first.

I am not suggesting here that a child should never learn right from wrong or hear the law taught in her home, because after all, "the law is holy, and the commandment is holy and righteous and good" (Romans 7:12), but I am suggesting that the law is not meant to be a tool to modify behavior so that 'right' behavior is the end goal but, instead, it is meant to be insight into the very nature of God and the heart of man. This theological concept is an important one for us all, as we understand that the law was never meant to save us, but to teach us our need for a Savior, and to reveal to us the depth of our sinfulness. When we realize this, we find hope, direction, guidance, and wisdom in the law, without the fear of punishment and the impossible goal of control or performance.

But when this isn't the case, and the law is used as a threat, then the child's relationship to the law changes. Rather than learning to love the law, their goal becomes avoiding its wrath. This avoidance of punishment is fueled by the flesh's desire for self-protection, not selflessness, and so it teaches our children to be selfish rather than selfless. If we want our children to understand a life of faith, then we've got to help them to get their eyes off of themselves and onto the Father. The tragic truth is that any obedience that we require of our children that is not motivated by the gospel breeds self-protection and self-obsession. But when the keeping of the law is motivated by love then selflessness is at the root of the behavior.

## An Imbalance of Law and Grace

I addressed it in the description of the authoritative parent in chapter two, but I want to tackle the issue of balance one more time. The gospel presents us with a conundrum, and that is one of an apparent balance of law and grace, as it offers us both 100% grace and 100% law but it's really quite imbalanced. It's 100% law in that the law exists and is inescapable. The law's purpose is to point us to our need for a Savior and cannot be overlooked. It is the presence of the law that reveals to us our sin and so cannot be minimized because to minimize it is to remove the need for a Savior. In order for there to be grace there has to first be the law, which reveals to us that we are all guilty.

But why even bother to up our grace/law quotient from 50/50 to 100/100? Aren't we saying the same thing? On the surface it might look like it, but let me explain. 50/50 is an inaccurate description of law and grace because 50/50 means half of the time grace is applied and the other half it's not. Imagine a judge, wanting to be balanced, waiving 50 percent of traffic violations each year, making it a flip of the coin whether a defendant will pay the fine or not. This method does no justice at all to the law that he is attempting to enforce. As Christian parents, it lays no foundation of grace as it leaves the guilty wondering "will they punish me for this today or let it slide?" In effect, it makes the role of judge and jury an emotional one, based on either how we feel or how much grace we have to spare.

But a change to 100% law and 100% grace, both/and, respects the law and removes the influence of the flesh. The law is ever-present and inescapable and grace, for the believer, is meant to be the same. But since the default for most of us is the law, as we look to it to help us to maintain order and control and to create obedient children, we have to learn to strategically think about the *intentional* and *liberal* application of grace.

The truth is that God's grace far outweighs the burden of our sin. Contrary to what our guilt might sometimes imply, *we cannot out-sin God's grace.* God's scale is always imbalanced with grace weighing far heavier in the life of faith than the burden of the law. Try to picture the scales of justice. On one side is all the paper (law) the pan can hold, 100% full (by volume). Now picture the other pan with all the gold it can hold; 100% full. The gold that is the grace of God will far outweigh the paper of the law (even if it was still written on stone tablets.) In the words of Charles Spurgeon, "There is more in the atonement by way of merit, than there is in all human sin by way of demerit."[viii]

**When children live under a 50/50 grace/law ratio, their lives become imbalanced and off-kilter because of the unpredictability of grace.** The question for them again becomes, "Is this the day I get punishment and severity or is it the day that I get forgiveness and grace?" It's basically a Russian Roulette of discipline and the most common response to this danger is an attempt to hide, cover up, and lie about mistakes and sins that may or may not lead to a negative outcome. But for your child to find stability there must be certainty that grace covers 100% of their failure. This imbalance of grace then means that rather than demerit accompanying every sin, Jesus' merit is right there to cover up the failure of not only us but also our children. The grace of God sets us all free from the sin that would otherwise condemn us. **So the question is, how do we apply that same grace we so freely embrace to the sins of our children?**

If we are honest with ourselves, the idea of free grace is a frightening one. It sounds too permissive and dangerous. It sounds like a rejection of the law and all that it stands for, and it sounds like a surefire way to create spoiled brats. Grace, we reason, isn't cheap and it can't be treated as if it were. It's the most expensive thing in the world, paid for by the priceless blood of the Lamb. And it's that expensive gift that's meant to cover all sin, not just sins of adults, but those of children as well.

What has first position in our minds as a parent: discipling our children in who Jesus is and who we are with and without him or disciplining, punishing, correcting, and training them into right behavior? When you embrace discipleship as your primary goal and job as parent, then discipline comes as a by-product of that discipleship. The gospel turns grammar upside down and discipleship becomes a verb and discipline becomes a noun. It comes through a building of the understanding of the gospel as it applies to the sin and salvation in their lives, and it comes as they learn just how much God loves them, just like it comes in your own life.

Discipleship for the adult is never about law and punishment. We don't grow in our faith because our discipler lays down the law and checks with us each week to see if we have kept it, and the punishment they might dole out when we fail to keep it wouldn't result in our spiritual growth. The concept is absurd, believing that discipleship is built on a foundation of discipline (the verb.) When you choose discipline as job one in your home then the best-case scenario is the 50/50 grace/law approach. But the approach of a house of grace in the message of the gospel is so much better.

### Allowing for Imperfection

As parents, our natural instinct is to want perfection for our kids. The new mom wants the perfect nursery. The new dad wants the perfect athlete. We naturally want our kids' environment, skills, and lives to be perfect. Even in the area of morality, obedience, and goodness, we want perfection for our kids and so we look for the benchmarks we can meet that not only keep us moving with the pack, but hopefully ahead of them in the area of perfection. When talking about raising perfect kids, our minds don't have to wander far before thinking about young sports prodigies or child stars that end up having secret or scandalous adult lives counter to the disciplined or moral way they were raised.

As a homeschooling family, it's easy for us to wonder about the perfection of the education our daughter is getting. A lot of times we sneak a peek at the standards set by educators to see just how wonderful or terrible we are doing in teaching her. If she (we) fail in meeting these benchmarks, we fear that we haven't done all we could be doing for her. And the same is true in the spiritual realm. The law is the benchmark we use to see if we've created a more perfect person than ourselves, believing that the keeping of the law will perfect our child or at least be some physical proof of her perfection. And so it's no surprise when we rely on either our own law or the law found in the scriptures, applying both without really applying the filter of the gospel.

Our natural instinct as a parent is to project perfectionism as the gospel that will save. In so doing we preach a gospel that we ourselves are unable to live up to. Inevitably, we end up discipling our child in something that we ourselves are not disciples of because we freely offer ourselves grace and excuse our own imperfections while not tolerating theirs. What occurs as we follow this path is that we begin to preach perfect obedience by pretending that we have it down while secretly living with the guilt and shame of falling short.

Unfortunately, it's natural to feel like our kids' imperfection reflect on our own imperfection and that's a scary place to be. And so it's extremely hard when our children misbehave in public, when they throw a fit, pull someone's hair, or knock someone down. The evidence of their imperfection is embarrassing and disheartening. And when they are even more spiritually imperfect and bully another kid, go too far sexually, or get caught using drugs or getting drunk then their behavior goes beyond embarrassment into humiliation and even self-accusation. The recording that starts running through our heads is, "what will they (friends, coworkers, church folk) think of me? Will they think I'm not a good parent? That I haven't taught my kids how to be godly? That I'm not a Christian?"

When Hayley was driving a friend of Addy's home one night, the little girl told her that her mommy yelled at her daddy a lot. Hayley cringed because she knows how the mom would feel if she heard herself talked about like that by her own child. She would be mortified! She is after all, a loving mother, who like any other woman loses her temper from time to time. But that doesn't lessen the sting of finding out that your child is telling people you're a shouter. When you have a little one in the house, all your privacy goes out the window and your life becomes an open book. But that doesn't necessarily change as they grow does it? Because as they grow, how they behave reflects on how you parent, and because of that it's easy to attempt to preach perfection, not only to save your child, but also to save yourself the social embarrassment.

The only way to parent with the same grace that God gives to us, is to offer our children the same grace God gives for our imperfections. If we demand perfection of our children to keep us looking good or to keep them faithful then we are already failures. And we are living under the self-deception that we can do what the Word of God says we cannot, create perfect followers of the law.

When we live in a house of perfection we live in a house of constant accusation. That's because the law, that defines perfection, is an accuser, and not an unfair one at that: they aren't trumped up charges. But because the law constantly accuses us, we tend to become accusers of others who aren't keeping the law as well as we think we are. We rationalize this because, after all, we all want something better for our kids, and so if it takes a 'scared straight' approach so they can avoid the same mistakes we made in our youth we will do it. Of course this is an exercise in futility and rooted in a prosperity gospel of parenting, which imagines that our kids deserve a better life than we had. But imagining that our kids will be perfect and never fall into sin is a gross mishandling and misrepresentation of the gospel.

Disciples are not made primarily on lecture, instruction, or discipline, but by observation of the discipler by the disciple. That means how we parent our child bears tremendous weight on the discipleship of our child.

In the time of Jesus, his disciples were called followers because they literally followed him around, listening to what he said and doing what he did. He was the one the disciples would imitate. So what then of the little disciples in our homes? Would it be a good thing or a bad thing for them to imitate us, to follow in our footsteps, to walk in our ways? Not to walk in the ways of our sin, but in the ways of our demand for perfection from others: not to walk in the ways of our past, but in the ways of our present?

This is the inherent danger of creating disciples of anyone but of Jesus himself. The only thing that we are qualified to be is a sinner saved by grace. If we want to disciple our kids to be perfect then we have to be living that way ourselves, otherwise we are telling them one thing and living another and that hypocrisy is then easily imitated by our kids who learn to live a double life just like we do.

The way we parent/disciple has to lead our children to a clear and biblical view of the gospel. And that means perfectionism can't be the goal, being successful can't be the goal, being well-mannered, being seen and not heard, turning out better than we did, being religious, patriotic, moral, none of these can be the goal. But to have a right view of God and of man, and a clear and intimate understanding of the gospel of grace, and to build a house that prodigals yearn to run back to, that is the goal of the discipling parent.

## Discipline is Not Discipleship

This leads us to an important distinction that must be embraced by every believing parent: discipline is not discipleship. Look at it like this, a parent can raise a disciplined child who follows all the rules but who is not a disciple of Christ. And this is easily the case when you fail to give them grace when they break the law. Believing that disobedience has to be punished, that there must be punitive consequences, creates an Old Testament environment for the children you are hoping to share the gospel with. To discipline a child and to believe that to be your primary shaping of their Christian identity (of your discipling them) is like stealing from someone you are sharing the gospel with. It makes your gospel words stand in stark contrast to your actions and, when this happens, your unconfessed hypocrisy obscures their view of God.

Punishment is the opposite of grace. Grace removes the punishment from the equation. But a lot of times it feels natural to punish your kids. So when you feel the need to punish ask yourself what motivates your desire. "Why do I want to punish? Is it to serve myself, my emotions, my anger, and my frustration? Is it retaliation? Vindication? Pursuit of perfection? And what does it teach them about grace?" Discipleship is non-existent when we discipline based on convenience or outrage, frustration or selfishness of any kind. In other words, we cannot discipline to relieve our stress or pressure, or to save ourselves time, money, energy, or embarrassment. Discipline should be meant to train our children first and foremost in the love and holiness of God, to nurture, mature, and aid them in growing in love and grace. And if grace has removed the need for punishment (Isaiah 53:5) then in an attempt to discipline our kids we need to remove the word 'punishment' from our vocabulary and its motivation from our motive, unless we want them transferring this idea to God and even onto themselves as they learn that punishment is needed for all of their mistakes. In these cases, young girls develop eating disorders, boys become bullies, and everyone fails to embrace the fact that Jesus took the punishment for our sins on himself, as we see in 1 Peter 2:24, "He himself bore our sins in his body on the tree, that we might die to sin and live to righteousness. By his wounds you have been healed." (1 Peter 2:24) His wounds are meant to be the topic of discipline not the wounds of the child. When we address their sin through the filter of his wounds it is an entirely different conversation and a more accurate portrayal of the gospel.

As adults we understand this idea of crime and punishment, but yet freely give ourselves the grace to commit the crime without receiving the punishment. For example, if you are speeding again and this time there is neither consequence nor punishment, do you determine that a price has to be paid for your transgression? If you say 'yes' then your next step upon seeing your speedometer go beyond its legal limit is to make a beeline for the police station where you will immediately confess your violation and proceed to the punishment of writing them a big fat check and voluntarily calling your insurance company for a rate adjustment.

## Consequences and Punishment

Most people freely interchange 'consequences' and 'punishment.' So I think that the difference needs to be examined. First off, consequences are circumstances that are either natural or created in response to an event. Now, created consequences *can be punitive* (*punishment,*) but they can also be gentle, harsh, heavy-handed, effective or ineffective depending on how they are communicated and the motivation behind the consequences.

Natural consequences are the things that naturally happen when we disobey or sin. But there is no such thing as natural punishment (with the exception of Hell perhaps.) We cannot confuse natural consequences with the consequences that we, as parents, create. For example, if you drive somewhere today and you go over the speed limit, there are some possible natural consequences for your infraction of the law. You can get into an accident, which includes the consequences of property damage, injury, or death. These are the possible natural consequences of breaking the law as a speeding driver. The possible created consequences in this scenario is the cost of a speeding ticket given by the officer that pulls you over or the higher insurance rate applied to you by your insurance company. Even punishment in the form of jail time for more severe accidents may be levied. Punishment is a type of created consequence meant to be punitive and to discourage you from breaking the law and compels you to settle a debt, while a natural consequence is a natural and common result of your action.

When I talk about the idea of punishment being inconsistent with grace most parents will reply, "but there have to be consequences!

How else will they learn their lesson and not do this thing again?" But natural consequences, those things that happen because of the action of sin, don't feel like punishment. Parents and other authority figures can create consequences that, when administered in grace, feel to the child less like punishment and more like loving discipleship. So, in order to help our kids maneuver through the rough terrain of sinful impulses, we have to learn how to allow for natural consequences over punishment and give them grace. If created consequences are needed, they have to be done in the spirit of love and discipleship and not punitive anger or frustration.

Four types of parents, natural and created consequences, discipleship versus punishment - let's see if we can put all these ideas together. I am a visual person, so let's see if the flow-chart on the next page will help you diagnose the approach you gravitate toward when faced with a disobedient child.

## HOW YOUR RESPONSE TO DISOBEDIENCE REVEALS YOUR PARENTING STYLE

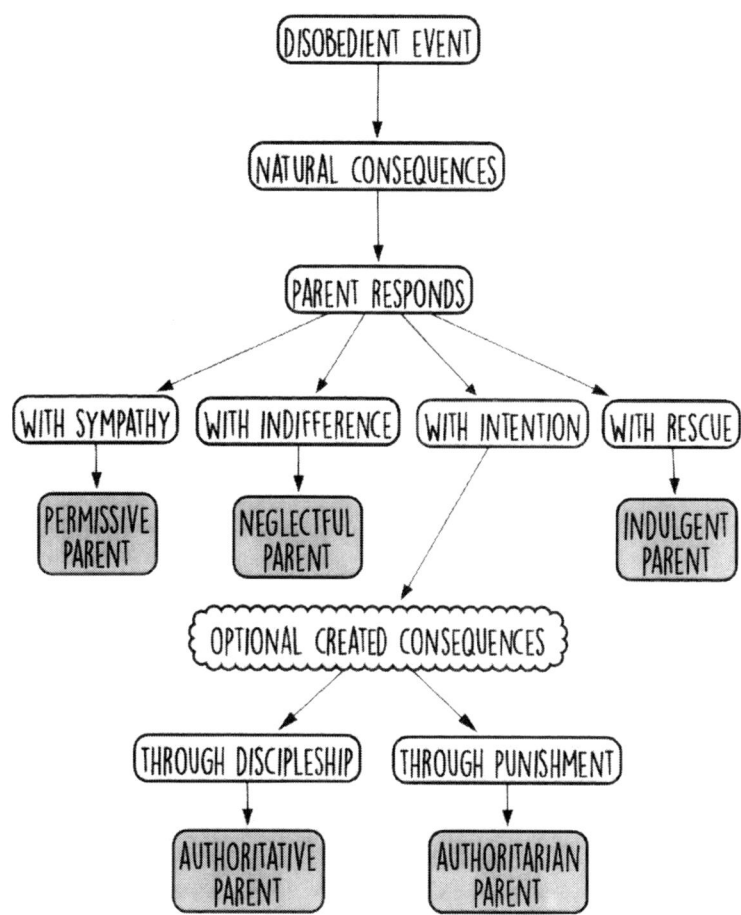

Following a disobedient event, natural consequences occur. If a child is rescued from those natural consequences, that is typical of an indulgent parent. If a parent responds to the child's disobedience and their suffering from the natural consequences with indifference, that is typical of the neglectful parent. If the parent responds to the disobedience and natural consequences with a sympathetic shoulder shrug of "oh well, what can you do," this can lead down the road of permissive or laissez-faire parenting. When a parent allows their child to experience natural consequences and walks them through those intentionally, through the motivation of discipleship, that is authoritative parenting. For the times that the natural consequences aren't enough, the parent creates additional consequences. If those are created through discipleship, then it is still authoritative parenting. But if the created consequences are used for punishment, or to "right" the behavior absent of grace or discipleship, then this leads to authoritarian parenting. An authoritative parent and authoritarian parent can create the exact same consequence for their child, the only differences are in the way they are administered, and the motive behind them.

Every time I hear an expert say "the one thing our kids want from us most is discipline" I cringe. Because let's be frank, ask one hundred kids, "what is the one thing you want from your parents?" and I guarantee you none will say discipline. This idea is a response by pastors and experts who realize that parents want disciplined children but don't want to put the work into making that happen. So, they created a blanket statement that might encourage the weak-hearted parent to offer their child some boundaries and rules to protect them. I believe this statement is only useful to the permissive or neglectful parent who shows no concern whatsoever for their unchecked child. Regardless, discipline still is not as powerful as the gospel and the grace through which it is given.

I believe that every child longs for a parent who cares enough to *disciple* them. Discipleship comes along side as one sinner to another and cares enough to guide the child through the pitfalls of life in love and grace. I've said this earlier, discipline is nose-to-nose and discipleship is shoulder-to-shoulder. Discipline is built upon power and subservience and can sow contempt, frustration, and rebellion. Discipleship builds imitation, relationship, and shared experience. That doesn't mean there won't be times of nose-to-nose, but they will be few and far between and the discipled child will need little explanation as to why the nose-to-nose moment occurred because of the deep trust and love that exists from the discipleship relationship.

In the words of Jerry Bridges, "God's grace is never conditional upon our performance." If it were it would fail to be grace. And so as grace receivers, we have got to reconsider the grace we withhold in favor of performance. Grace doesn't come when the child is good, like a cookie from the cookie jar that we put up on top of the refrigerator just out of their reach so that we can get into it whenever we want, but they can only have access when we think they deserve it. Grace comes when we are in the midst of the messing up; in our sin grace comes. As it says in Romans 5:6-9):

*"For while we were still weak, at the right time Christ died for the ungodly. For one will scarcely die for a righteous person—though perhaps for a good person one would dare even to die— but God shows his love for us in that while we were still sinners, Christ died for us. Since, therefore, we have now been justified by his blood, much more shall we be saved by him from the wrath of God."*

So the cookie jar of grace is accessible and offered when offenses occur, rather than only after obedience has been displayed.

In 1 John 2:2 we read, *"He is the propitiation for our sins, and not for ours only but also for the sins of the whole world."* And in 1 John 4:10 we read: *"In this is love, not that we have loved God but that he loved us and sent his Son to be the propitiation for our sins."* Jesus bore the punishment for our sins if we merely confess and repent. So there should be no double jeopardy for us or our children. This means that parenting under the Old Testament law has to be redeemed through this payment. So we parent/disciple not with the law in mind but out of the grace that we first received. It's a whole new world of parenting based on loving our children as empathetic sinner-parents saved by grace.

The propitiation for our sin should encourage parents to remember how we used to parent based on the Old Testament, and remind us that we no longer have to punish our children in order to save them. *They will never be good enough.* But thanks be to God that he sent his Son for us all, kids included. This means if their Heavenly Father's wrath has been satisfied, so should ours as their earthly parents. In a way, your child will love as he or she is first loved by you.

If the desired result of your parenting is a disciplined child, you are going to default to a posture of nose-to-nose parenting, either in an authoritarian or gospel-less authoritative style. If the desired end result of your parenting is discipleship, you will tend toward a shoulder-to-shoulder position that is gentle, humble, and builds relationship. The nose-to-nose nature of discipline is built upon harshness, performance, pride, and individual power. That's why discipline, especially certain forms of it, has a shelf life; it's not sustainable once the child has equal or more power than you do. The child gaining power and independence over you could be because they outgrew you or they just don't need your money anymore. Because discipleship isn't built on the foundation of power but of relationship, as the relationship grows so then does the discipleship. Discipleship teaches not through ultimatums and law but through grace, through shared experiences of a big sinner with a little sinner. When discipleship is the focus, and relationship has been the foundation, which the discipleship has been built upon, the times nose-to-nose discipline occurs become very rare and very brief.

## Discipleship builds self-discipline

He became a believer at 32. He had a hard life. He had lived in sin for many years. When he met Jesus, he was a changed man, at least on the inside. His outside took awhile to join in on the transformation. And so he went to church on Sundays and the bar on Mondays. He loved God but was a spiritual baby in adult clothes. One day someone suggested he find a man who could disciple and teach him how to live as a believer. At their first meeting the 'accountability partner' gave him a list of rules, things that would make his life better, more holy and more acceptable to God. Things like don't get drunk, don't smoke, don't cuss, and don't sleep around. You know, the usual faire for the born again partier.

When they met the next week, unfortunately, our friend didn't have much success to report. It started out good with him going out with some of his buddies. He told them his testimony and talked about his new life. But then they wanted him to have a drink, and he thought he'd have just one. Then they bought a few more rounds, invited some girls over to their table, and muscle memory took over. Before he knew it, he woke up in some girl's apartment. What a mess!

Later that week, after he confessed his mess, his discipler stood up and paced the room, hands on his head. What to do with a complete failure who had done everything on the "don't do" list? The discipler turned around and said in a stern voice, "Okay, well, it's clear to me that you need help, so I am going to give you some consequences for your sin. Since you did what you knew you shouldn't, I am going to take away your driver's license for the next week so you can't go to bars. Hand it over! I guess I'm going to have to drive you everywhere so you won't 'mess up.' I don't know what else I can do to disciple you into a real saving faith. You just can't seem to do it on your own."

I'd like to say that this never happened, but I hear similar stories to this more times than I can count. Hopefully the reaction of the discipler seems counter-intuitive to you. This is a strange take on the work of the Holy Spirit in the life of faith. Punishment does not make disciples. Punishment only discourages and accuses of guilt, it doesn't transform.

In this scenario, the discipler taught the law, which our friend needed to understand, but then he took that law to be the tool that would accomplish an internal change in our friend. Unfortunately, what the law doesn't accomplish is heart change. The threat of law enforcement teaches us a standard of what we need to do in order to be accepted, to be approved, and to be safe. But at the root of all of those desires is self. So at the root, proving yourself by the law is attempting to do what is necessary in order to save self, to be your own savior by the fruit of your own effort, and won't produce holy self-discipline (self-control) but self-interested obedience.

When we train, correct, and parent using the threat of punishment, the other person's obedience is fueled by fear, protection, self-interest, or a combination of the three. It isn't fueled by love for the Father, but love for self, and avoidance of pain and punishment. This doesn't teach us self-discipline and mindfulness of the sin in our life, but mindlessness and rote memory as we learn exactly what must be said in order to be saved. It doesn't teach reliance on the Holy Spirit, but on the performance of necessary actions and the avoidance of dangerous ones. Of course the law of discipline might make obedient kids who do what they are told, but it doesn't make selfless disciples who practice self-discipline as they respond to the promptings of the Spirit.

In a house of grace, self-discipline is taught and fed by a preponderance of grace, not discipline. You can easily create an obedient and pliable child who rejects the savior. But you cannot raise a disciple of Christ who rejects God's law. Read that one again. You can easily create an obedient and pliable child who rejects the savior, but you cannot raise a disciple of Christ who rejects God's law. By definition, a disciple of Christ cherishes the law. As we cherish our God we want what he wants, not in order to protect ourselves from His or anyone else's wrath but in order to give him glory. Disciples of Christ are self-disciplined, not through fleshly effort but through holy surrender, because they reject self and their own will and want only God and His perfect will. So this begs the question, do your little disciples see a surrender of self in you to mimic, are they simply being legislated into their own selflessness?

The truth is that discipline for the sake of compliance is enslaving, but grace for the sake of discipleship is freedom from the bondage of sin. After all, what frees us from sin's dominion? Law or grace? For the answer to that let's take a look at Romans 6:14, "For sin will have no dominion over you, since you are not under law but under grace." Sin has no dominion because of grace; therefore sin loses its power under grace, but conversely gains it under a system of law alone.

The law is important; it teaches us what God cherishes and what he hates and makes sin utterly sinful (see Romans 7:13). It reveals our own sin to us (see Romans 3:20) and shows us our need for a Savior (see Galatians 3:21-22). But it was never meant to save us. It is powerless to save and, in fact, actually serves to increase our sin (see Romans 5:20). If we want to address our children's disobedience biblically then we have to see any disobedience as a chance to teach them the purpose of the law, which isn't to make our family run more smoothly or our kids to act more politely. It is to reveal our need for God and his grace more deeply.

The conviction that leads the child to respond to the Spirit rather than the law is developed not solely by memorization and study of the law, but by seeing it applied in real life situations. As they see God's law acted out in front of them they understand it and learn it, but not only that, they act upon it. But who can blame them; they are merely copying whatever it is they see in you. If they experience a graceless set of laws, they will respond in that same gracelessness to the law giver, and out of that will come the terrible teen years when your young adult begins to set their gracelessness against yours. And the battle is on.

Unlike discipline, discipleship teaches discernment. Give a kid a fish or teach a kid to fish? Parents confuse teaching their kids what to do and what not to do with teaching them how to fish. The reality is that most parents are just teaching them how to behave so that they can get a fish. They withhold the fish until the child complies and then they give them the fish. But teaching a child to fish isn't about telling them what they can and can't do. It goes beyond talking about why they should or shouldn't do something and goes to the heart of why they would want to do something. The discipling parent digs down to the sinful heart of man both in what he wants and in what he is afraid to risk. And they teach their child how to fish, especially when this teaching on the depravity of man is combined with the phrase, 'but God.' 'But God' says, "cast out all fear," and "with God all things are possible."

Discipleship teaches discernment, it leads to self-discipline. In other words, it leads to a morality not fed by fear, pride, or rote memory, but rooted in knowing who we are both as fallen sinners and as heirs; adopted sons and daughters of the most high God. "Teaching a child to fish" is synonymous with "teach a child to be self-disciplined" and that's the essence of discernment. Discernment from discipleship is not rooted in what to do and what not to do, but in abiding in Christ, his words, and his Spirit. In this frame of mind we then seek out spiritual discipline and desire obedience not for fear of punishment but for the joy we receive when we give God glory.

## Disobedience: The Opportunity for Discipleship

For most of us, the disobedience of our children feels like an indictment on our parenting skills or, at the very least, like a trip to the emergency room; it can be a major inconvenience to our plans for the day. Let me suggest that when we parent with grace, disobedience becomes simply another opportunity to share the gospel with our children. That's the key to discipleship (parenting;) it's seeing every sinful act as an opportunity to teach. It is, after all, failure that is the best teacher because it allows us entry into the hearts of our children; it's the time when they will most likely listen to us. So why waste your kid's disobedience by merely punishing the behavior when you could spend it on revealing the nature of the heart of man (and sharing your own heart's sinful condition.) For the discipling parent, disobedience is a far more valuable opportunity to disciple and share the gospel of grace than to punish and extract right behavior.

In his book *The Discipline of Grace* Jerry Bridges writes,

"All our efforts to teach godly living and spiritual maturity to others must be grounded in grace. If we fail to teach that discipline is by grace, people will assume, as I did, that it is by performance. That is why we must not put the gospel on the shelf once a person becomes a new believer. He or she will have just as difficult a time believing that God relates to us every day on the basis of grace as a person has believing that God saves by grace instead of works. So we must not only preach the gospel to ourselves every day, we must continue to teach it and preach it to those whom we may be discipling in some way, whether in a Sunday school class or Bible study we are teaching or in a one-to-one mentoring relationship. Discipleship must be based on Gods' grace." (Pg. 81-82. Jerry Bridges, the Discipline of Grace)

It is unfortunate that there is no reference to parenting or children in this solid and gospel-rich approach to discipleship, but there should be! This idea that the gospel communicated is more important than the law obeyed is essential for each one of us as individual believers, and as parents, to understand.

When we don't embrace grace in parenting, we usually fail to teach the sinfulness of the heart of man, and of our own hearts, to our children. When we fail to teach the sinfulness of our hearts we fail to teach the gospel. When we don't embrace grace we fail to teach the powerlessness of the law to save us. If we fail to teach the powerlessness of the law, our children learn to spend their lives attempting the impossible; saving themselves through performance. The end result may be addiction, depression, discontentment, fear, anger, and possibly more issues. Do not take these words lightly. The troubles your children will face find their roots in their failure to understand or accept the gospel message. We all have sinned and will continue to sin causing us to be separated from God. The only thing that will bring us back into right relationship with him is a relationship with his Son Jesus Christ, not by works, not by obedience, and not by good deeds.

Therefore, it is reasonable to say that the obedience that we all long for in our children is best found not in our enforcement of the law but in delivering His grace on the heels of their breaking that law. In other words, their disobedience is an opportunity for discipleship and for sharing of the gospel. But be warned, this approach of grace isn't always as swift as discipline, and therefore, when you first start out it can seem cumbersome, time consuming, and wholly unsatisfying to our flesh. Give it some time because the more you practice this style of parenting the more quickly your children recover and make changes in their choices, not out of fear but out of the love and grace you display as a parent.

Let's take a look at an example. Let's say your child has lied to you about breaking your cellphone. The swiftest route would be to take away something she loves - i.e. punishment. Janey lies and so you take away her iPod for a week and she learns her lesson, right? Well, that's the swiftest way to get the justice you want and to release some of your pent up frustration. Parenting isn't about expediency and justice, but about teaching your child to love God with all her heart, soul, and mind. Punishment will not accomplish this, but taking her sinful act as an opportunity to reveal God's goodness and grace will.

So how does it work? When Janey lies about breaking your phone that she wasn't supposed to have been playing with, the discipling choice is to talk about the gospel. The focus should be on the idea of deception. What is it in us, not just her but us as humans, that leads us to lie? Talk about how Satan lied to Eve and how she lied to herself and Adam. Why do we lie? What does this teach us about our relationship with God? The conversation might go something like this:

Dad: *Why did you lie about what you did? What did you fear?*

Janey: *I was afraid that you would be mad at me.*

Dad: *The most important thing to me isn't that you disobeyed, we all disobey, the Bible says 'there is no one righteous, not even one.' But the most important thing is that you know the way out of your mistake isn't more mistakes or hiding, but confession. If we confess our sins, God is faithful and will forgive our sins, but they can't be forgiven while we lie about them or hide them. I will always love you, no matter how much you lie or mess up. I want you to know that, just like God, when you confess your mistakes I will still love you and love always forgives.*

The biggest challenge of situations like these is skipping past anger or stress into discipleship. If we're angry about the phone shattering, we won't disciple. If we're stressed about where to get the money to replace it, we're displaying to our child we're unsure that God will provide. If we respond out of fear our child is becoming a klutz, we'll reinforce a culture of performance in our home. Most parents fear the failure of their kids more than anything else, but my wife and I have no fear of Addy's failure or her sin because we see each mistake in her life as confirmation of the gospel and the best opportunity in the world to reveal to her more about the character of God as seen in the life of Jesus Christ. The most important thing we as parents can teach our kids is who we are naturally, in our flesh, and who we are because of God. The message of the gospel is that because we have sinned we have a need for a Savior. This is something we need to preach to ourselves as well as our children every time that we sin.

We don't have to get all cleaned up to accept his grace. We simply have to recognize our need for it. Giving our children an environment where grace is more important than perfection. Allowing them to be human while teaching them that failure will happen, but that we still love them the same way God still loves all of us who fail. This allows the law to be something that revives the soul and enlightens the eyes to the need for a Savior, rather than something to use to our advantage or to run from.

### The Danger of the God Complex

In the beginning our love created a child. And the child was good. And the child could do no wrong. There was a playpen, or a swing, and her fat legs couldn't carry her. In the first year there was crawling and then walking, and the rug was good. Then there was food, and there was juice, and everything was permissible except juice on the white rug. One day while the child was drinking purple juice and the purple dinosaur was singing on the TV, the white rug looked good to dance upon. So, she danced onto the rug and the juice sloshed and slid over the sides of the cup and onto the rug. Suddenly the child could see and she was scared, and she ran into her room and hid so that her mother would not find her.

What we do next in this situation depends on two questions:
1. What kind of parent we are (four kinds of parents)?
2. What is our view on the purpose of parenting (discipleship or something else)?

But when the juice spills on the rug there's a key moment where we reveal our position in relationship to the spiller. Are we the creator and the rug is the tree in the middle of the garden? If so, then swift action will soon follow because amends must be made, laws must be enforced. In most of our homes the lawgiver is understood to be us as parents instead of God himself. We espouse morality in our children and homes and expect our kids to grow up as Bible-believing adults. As representatives of the law of God, we easily run the risk of falling into a parenting condition I call 'the god complex.' When grace isn't the automatic reaction to failure, law is and law requires justice, but law also requires a lawgiver.

For example, the well-known verse for children to, 'honor your father and your mother and you will have a long life' (see Exodus 20:12) is now paraphrased to go more like this, 'parents make sure your kids honor you.' After all, we want everything to go well with our kids, as the commandment promises, so we think we've got to make sure they follow the law. Because this is one of the few commands in the Bible that refers to parents, we make it about us. But this verse isn't written to the parents, it's written to the kids. Adult kids specifically, according to Jesus who says, *"For example, God said, 'Honor your father and your mother' and 'Whoever curses father or mother must be put to death.' But you say that whoever tells his father or mother, 'I have given to God whatever support you might have received from me,' does not have to honor his father. Because of your traditions you have destroyed the authority of God's word."* (Matthew 15:4–6, GWT) Jesus clearly applies this commandment to adult children who have failed to support their elderly parents. In multiple commentaries, including Nelson's New

Illustrated Bible Commentary, the authors agree by saying that, "care of one's elderly parents was a basic element of social responsibility and godly piety in Israel. Here [Exodus 20:12] it is directly tied to how a person would fare in the land. People who were faithless to God in disregarding their parents would not last long in the new Promised Land." But when we take a verse and demand others keep it, rather than applying it to ourselves, we are not obeying the law but using it in order to get what we want. It would be like a wife demanding that her husband love her, a command that is clearly meant for him, and punishing him (or withholding love herself) if he didn't obey.

When Hayley and I were first married I was often angry with her for not loving me the way I wanted to be loved and I passive-aggressively took it out on her. Similarly, when I failed to show her kindness and joy, she resented me for my sinful failings and punished me in various non-violent ways. Needless to say, our first year of marriage was a romantic disaster, but one thing learned, eventually, was that God's Word isn't meant to be enforced by the offended party, but applied to each one of us through the Holy Spirit. Just allow my and Hayley's failure in sharing grace with one another as spouses to be an example of the same failure we exercise devotedly in our parent/child relationships.

It's subtle, but stick with me, when we take God's Word and wield it as a demand for others to treat us a certain way we begin to develop a god complex that makes demands on others that we were never meant to make.

It can be easy to look at God's commands not as how we are to treat our children, but how they are to treat us. The law was written to each of us as individual believers telling us what God expects of us, not what we are to enforce in others. Only in the rare occasion of church discipline does God's Word lead us to demand others to comply with the law. The majority of scripture is meant to inform the reader of their own obligations to love God with all their heart and to love their neighbors as themselves. When we take what God commands of us and enforce it on others, as in "you better honor me," or "the Bible says you have to turn your cheek when I slap you," this backwards way of thinking makes us the god who enforces the law rather than the disciple who follows it. As parents, wouldn't we be more faithful to ask ourselves "do I honor my parents?" And, "am I living a life that is easily honored by my children?"

Obviously, I am not suggesting that the law be thrown out and we not teach our children God's precepts, what I am saying is that somewhere along the way we have failed to believe that God's law is meant for us. Instead we have majored on law enforcement, both of God's law and of our own. God's law is what is his written Word, and we all understand that it is good and perfect, but with that law comes complete grace to cover our offenses. But what of our own laws? How do we enforce those things that we deem as necessary for the health and welfare of our family? Things like mealtime or bedtime behavior, noise levels, kindness, and chores? How do we enforce these 'essentials' when grace is the prescription? Or is there any grace needed for these kinds of laws?

The truth is that God's law and a parent's laws aren't always synonymous; scripture doesn't legislate when a child has to remove her shoes or how much time is allowed in front of the TV. So many well-meaning parents keeps extending "honor your father and mother" into an endless list of honor inducing, God-ordained do's and don'ts that are really based on manners, parental preference, and moralism instead of the gospel of grace.

Don't get me wrong; I am not rejecting family rules all together. I am just trying to point out the unnoticed fact that our family rules (laws) are often given equal if not greater weight than God's laws, all under the enforcement of 'honor your parents!' When that happens it's either evidence of or fuel for the god complex whereby we insist that our kids do as we tell them because we are parents meant to be honored!

In reality, most of our difficulty with our children comes from their difficulty with our laws not God's. God's laws can certainly be a challenge for us all, especially those that deal with us dying to ourselves, but truth be told our parental laws cause the most strife. That's because when our laws are broken we are the most inconvenienced and the flesh doesn't like that at all. The laws that we create to keep order in our home and protect our stuff might serve our family good enough, but most of the time they are really all about serving ourselves, making our lives easier.

For example, one day Addy asked Hayley for chicken nuggets for breakfast. Hayley's first response was an emphatic 'no,' we don't eat chicken nuggets for breakfast. Addy was sad because that's what she had her heart set on. After I shot her a quizzical look, Hayley reminded herself that this wasn't a biblical mandate but a human custom that she was following out of habit. There was no reason she couldn't give her chicken nuggets, it wouldn't change anything in their day. In fact, it was easier than making eggs and bacon or pancakes. So she walked over to our daughter and apologized to her for enforcing a law that wasn't truly a law. "We can eat lunch for breakfast; God has no law against that. I'm sorry I jumped on you as if you broke the law. Sometimes I forget what really matters," she said and hugged Addy's neck. Then she prepared her lunch for breakfast and all was well. Our child learned not only the beauty of self-correction and honest confession but also of rejecting the development of our own law at the expense of loving others. And later that evening she discovered the ultimate nugget of God's common grace to humans, pancakes and bacon for dinner!

As parents, it's only natural to create boundaries for our kids so that as they grow they are safe, but quite easily these boundaries can start to become law to us, if only subconsciously. We then find ourselves more committed to our 'law' than to God's. We get frustrated when our rules aren't followed, when our plans are interrupted, when little hands break our stuff or mess up our system. We rely on the law to prove that our frustration and even anger is just, without considering the fact that not only is our anger not justified, but also our 'law' is not God's law. Even if it were, when we react in anger to little lawbreakers, we act with more judgment than the God of mercy, himself. When we begin to believe that our law is just that, 'law,' we reject grace as an attack against our plans, our beliefs, and our desires. We react with frustration and harshness as we try to redirect our kids into a more comfortable and convenient path for us.

It's like this, if my child is having fun playing with a big Lego project and I say it's time to put this mess away because it's bedtime. She responds by saying, 'but I'm not done with it, I can't put it away.' I say, 'sorry, everything has to be put away at bedtime,' I have just made my own made-up-law-of-order more important than my child and her plans, her work, her enjoyment. I have just said that my 'need' for order is more important than her 'need' to complete her project. This doesn't go unnoticed. The child might not be able to label it right then and there as the idol of self, but believe me they have learned it, 'order is more important than I am.' Their heart records it, and the 'love bank' as some would call it, has another withdrawal.

You might ask, "How can we teach our kids the law if we don't judge their actions, pass a verdict, and give a suitable punishment? Justice, after all, is in our hands as the chief executors of the law for our kids. Offering grace to strangers, sure, I get it, but offering grace to our kids? That seems unsafe and downright dangerous to our position of power as a parent, as well as to their development as obedient and moral followers." Deuteronomy 6 pretty much sums it up:

*"And these words that I command you today shall be on your heart. You shall teach them diligently to your children, and shall talk of them when you sit in your house, and when you walk by the way, and when you lie down, and when you rise. You shall bind them as a sign on your hand, and they shall be as frontlets between your eyes. You shall write them on the doorposts of your house and on your gates." (Deuteronomy 6:6–9)*

Yes, Deuteronomy does sum up the life of faith, talking about the things of God 24/7, but when I see how most parents speak to their kids I fail to find much of God in it at all. Phrases like:

"Do as I say, not as I do."

"Because I said so!"

"Children shall be seen and not heard."

"You are going to respect me."

"Because this is my house!"

None of these are part of God's law, but of man's. The pathology behind all of this to the child's ears is, 'you don't matter yet,' and 'I shouldn't have to explain myself to you.' It all points to the god complex that says, 'my ways are not your ways.'

This all starts when, as parents of extremely small children, we fall in love with our power, ability, and necessity to dictate their entire lives. Ok, maybe it's not us falling in love with the power but out of a survival instinct. During these tender years full power is required, but as they grow and we fail to loosen our deity grip, we continue the same pattern established for the baby into toddler, elementary, and even high school years.

Now we have the god complex that requires that we discipline nose-to-nose in order to maintain control and we never move into the shoulder-to-shoulder walk of discipleship. This walk requires more of our non-stop time and energy outlined in Deuteronomy 6 and is often sacrificed on the altar of convenience choosing to opt out of the long conversations of why we do what we do, why we fail, and what it all means. Instead, we choose the quick fix that the law, both biblical and familial, allows.

I know a lot of believers who, in relationship to others who aren't in their family, are very biblically minded. They are humble, kind, and patient. They might not always get it all right but they have a deep desire to apply all of God's Word to their lives except that one area remains out of bounds to that Berean way of thinking and that is the area of parenting. When I have offered them help with their children, they have been surprised to hear me apply the entirety of God's Word and not just the few verses on parenting.

For example, when a parent continues to remind their child of their past disobedience, to use it as a weapon against them in the war of obedience, I remind them "love keeps no record of wrongs." They have a hard time making the connection in relationship to disciplining their kids. "But it's my job to keep records of their wrongs," they argue. Then should God have made an exception to his teaching on love, one that applies to people under the age of eighteen? Or just to people who are younger than you or reliant on you for survival? What are the edits that you want to make to God's Word?

When the child, through repeated practice, comes to understand their position in your heart, your position in theirs takes a hit, and learning by observation as they do, their obsessions start to crowd you out in their life. Why do parents of teens find so much anger and distance building in their relationship with their children? Probably because they have been unknowingly contributing to it by repeatedly revealing their own idols to their children.

The answer to this human tendency to think of ourselves first is to continually assess our own motives. When we dig deep and see that our main motive in disciplining our child is ultimately about our comfort, performance, peace, or neuroses, then the motive is selfishness. There is always a choice, either our motive is us and our "needs" or it is love. If it is love, then there will be many, many times when attention, play, and joy will take precedence over order, cleanliness, peace, and quiet.

One mother I know was bent on teaching her children to be responsible, and so she created a rule that when she put their clean clothes on their bed, they had to be put away by the end of day. If they were not, she boasted with a smile, that she would come in and pick them up and give them away to charity. This happened daily until they learned to put their clothes away promptly. Practically, this might sound like a good idea to you! You might want to start trying that style of parenting, but before you do, consider the motive behind this way of disciplining. The first motive isn't to glorify or bring joy to God, but to the parent who dislikes having to pick up after the child or look at a messy room. The second motive is to get the child to obey out of fear of losing something that matters to her. This helps to keep her on her toes, quick to listen and obey, just like God commands, right? No, this form of control smacks of the god complex whereby the parent's desires, not God's, becomes the law for the child. As stated earlier, contrary to popular belief, there is no verse that tells us that cleanliness is next to godliness. A Berean, one who checks their own motives and actions against God's Word, would know this. Any attempt to insist that your child honor you by doing what you want so that they will honor God in the process hijacking his commandment. God has not made this a command, nor asked you to enforce it.

This isn't to say that we cannot expect our kids to clean up their messes and to put things away. The law of discipline attaches to this training the fear of punishment, which becomes more impactful than what the message should be behind the act. The message should be biblically driven which would be cleaning up is a part of servanthood, caring more for others than for self, and this is always best learned by *example*, not by threats. A decade or so ago a popular question was often asked, "What would Jesus do?" A lot of us used this as a divining rod, helping us to know how to act in situations where we weren't sure what to do. For example, in the case of servanthood, Jesus gave us a great picture. He didn't just command his disciples to serve, but served them as he washed their feet (see John 13:1-17). This idea of washing feet is the lowest of lows. Dirty, stinky feet, weary from travel, dirty from the dust and grime that had easy access because of primitive footwear, and Jesus knelt there face-to-feet. Knowing this, can you see Jesus coming into your room and yelling at you to clean it up? Or does this example suggest that, if there is an expectation that you clean your room, he might just come in and clean up your room for you or alongside you and telling you why he's doing it?

A parent that wants to disciple their child to clean up can explain to them that they are getting old enough now to do this or that, making the task a privilege rather than a drag. Add to that being a cheerleader, encouraging growth and achievement. We cheerlead a lot in our home and I am *not* a cheerleader by nature; I am a born critic. Grace replaces chastising or shaming them when they fail. That means that we offer them the grace of assistance, mercy, and of understanding what it's like to be a kid filled with the joy and excitement of making a mess, having limited responsibility and enjoying this time for all that it is worth before the burdens of life start to pile up. The grace of discipleship in this scenario makes the bed for the child who forgets or creates a fun game of it and uses it as an example of God's grace given to us who don't deserve it. This is not to curry favor but to obey Christ who said, "*But whoever would be great among you must be your servant, and whoever would be first among you must be slave of all. For even the Son of Man came not to be served but to serve, and to give his life as a ransom for many*" (Mark 10:43–45).

My wife and I endeavor to demonstrate grace to others in front of our daughter on as many occasions as possible. Guess what she ends up copying? That's right, becoming a grace-giver. These words make it clear, unless we are to believe that "all" excludes a certain class, race, age, or gender of people, we have got to apply this concept to our children as well. It is funny how easily the average believer will grab hold of and tout the importance of becoming a servant the way Christ taught us through his own example but will reject this very precept when it comes to their children. In our homeschool co-op, all the kids and parents come together once a week. At lunchtime, Addy becomes a pied piper to the littles (all the kids littler than her.) This is not because she doesn't have good friends her own age or we tell her to, it's because they are looking for someone to help with their games, and she remembers us doing the same for her.

We often forget that when the Bible was written, women and children were considered possessions or property of the family patriarch. They were not given the same rights as men, and so these concepts were just as revolutionary to those of Jesus' time as they are to the parents of our time, but that doesn't make them any less applicable. Christ came to change the game. How can we claim to worship a Christ whose example we are afraid to follow for fear of losing control, power, or order in the home?

This idea is revolutionary because we've allowed the word of God to exclude children for so long that we can't conceive of including them in commands like, "Do nothing from selfish ambition or conceit, but in humility count others more significant than yourselves" (Philippians 2:3–4). Many of us might believe that we consider our children more significant than ourselves, but any time that we put ourselves and our self-interest over theirs we prove otherwise. We do this when we put them on a pedestal and obsess over them and also when we harshly discipline them. Both of these reflect a god complex that makes this life all about ourselves, our joy, hope, hard work, dreams, and feelings. By doing this, we fail to accept God's Word and begin to write our own "law."

For many parents, the god complex reveals our need for justice. Justice is written on our hearts. Instinctually we know there is right and wrong, fair and unfair, but the trouble with this comes when we believe that justice is meant to be carried out by man instead of God. God seeks to be gracious to us as it says in Isaiah 30:18, *"Yet the LORD longs to be gracious to you; he rises to show you compassion. For the LORD is a God of justice. Blessed are all who wait for him!"* It can be very easy when your child fails you, especially in front of the eyes of others, to skip right over grace and kindness and to feel the full brunt of hurt and embarrassment. It's easy to take their failure as an attack or an indictment on you. When you let those feelings grow, it's easy to demand justice and that's when tempers start to flare, rules get enforced, and punishment gets doled out. In these heated moments the grace you received from God fades into the background and your law screams for discipline. Trouble is, when you discipline out of self-protection you make yourself the god who was offended, and the god complex builds in your home.

But many might say, "I'm just standing up for the offenses against God." That might be true, but isn't the goal of discipling to teach your child how to act when they see sin in their lives, not for you to act as a god in their lives? The first reaction to sin should be confession like we see in the life of David who said, "against you [God] alone have I sinned and you alone" (see Psalm 51:4.)

Okay, this might seem like a 'duh' moment, but think about it, it's far more important as the discipler to our children to teach them how to be a disciple than how to be God. The role we are preparing them for isn't to become another deity, but another sinner following

Christ. Our god complex seemingly promises to serve us well as we attempt to become more Christ-like by becoming more God-like, and the idea of being god to your children is a wrong one, another "duh" moment, I know. It needs to be said, because truthfully how many of us think this way? Shepherding your child the way Christ shepherded the church is the goal of the grace of discipleship, not becoming a perfect judge to them.

## A Sheep With a Shepherd's Heart

Familiar imagery in the scriptures is that of shepherd and sheep. We predominately see this in church life where the pastor is called the "shepherd of the flock," but we also hear that the parent should be a shepherd to their children. The shepherd guides his sheep, leading them to what they require; green grass, clean water, and a safe place to lie down. He protects them with his rod, which is used to reach out and guard them from going in the wrong direction and to fight off wolves intent on snatching up the young lambs. Sheep require a shepherd because they cannot take care of or protect themselves.

Unfortunately, the pastor/parent/shepherd is often unfairly elevated to the level of super-human or super-saint by their flock, if not by themselves. The idea of knowing more, of being more educated, powerful, discerning, and 'spiritual,' can feed the god complex in the life of a shepherd. For the shepherd, the danger that comes with this idea is that he can't be real, have flaws, or confessions of sin, and that creates pressure and isolation for him. Instead of getting an empathetic and authoritative leader who has already walked the valleys the flock is walking, we get a sympathetic, removed, or authoritarian 'higher' life form that can never ultimately relate to us. Instead of getting community, we get isolation and distortion, the distortion of the true condition of the shepherd. The inherent problem is that we have sheep playing dress up, sheep in shepherd's clothing. Even though we know that pastors are sheep, that *we as parents are sheep*, we get lost in the game of playing dress up and see whoever is dressed up as a shepherd as having the omnipotent, opposable thumbs of a higher being instead of the fallible, clumsy hooves of a sheep. Rather, I as a parent should never pretend to be anything more than a sheep with a shepherd's heart; I am to be just another sinner with the wounds and scars and stories of God's grace and how it saved and is continually saving me. If we look at our pastor and we only see a shepherd and not his 'sheepishness,' then we see someone with no need for grace and therefore someone who can neither suffer with us nor understand us. How many parents have heard this complaint from their kids, "you just don't understand me?" The disconnection and isolation they feel is because we are too afraid to show ourselves for who we really are, sheep tasked with shepherding duties in equal need of grace that comes from the Great Shepherd. This fear gives way to separation, as we become the ideal they repeatedly fail to reach.

So, how do we shepherd those who are less spiritual than us without isolating ourselves and feeding our god complex? The answer is to become an authority on being a sheep, in other words, on having lots of experience needing and receiving God's grace. So, instead of cracking the whip, the wise shepherd cracks the example. When we parent out of the fear of our children becoming sinners, instead of parenting out of the reality that indeed our children are born sinners, we fail to embrace the need for daily grace. This paradigm shift is one of the most freeing facts about spiritual parenting. That is, instead of living in fear of what already is, we can live in victory for what Christ has already done. This is the basis of a gospel-centered house of grace. Again and again I tell you, Romans 3:10-12 reminds us of this very important fact, *"None is righteous, no, not one; no one understands; no one seeks for God. All have turned aside; together they have become worthless; no one does good, not even one."* Believing that your child is born pure and that you have to guard their purity, keeping them sin-free or all is lost is a misconception that haunts many parents, but that way of thinking is pointless and destructive.

Here are four more ways that adopting the parenting philosophy, "big sinners raising little sinners" fundamentally changes your home into a house of grace:

1. Removes the emotional "surprise" from disobedience.
2. Creates empathy, community, and closeness.
3. Moves discipline from reactionary moments to a lifelong journey.
4. Moves discipline from nose-to-nose to shoulder-to-shoulder.

When we see our kids as little sinners who need to learn from us big sinners, we find ourselves more freely able to give them the grace that God gives us. When they fail, and they will, we won't take it personally, fly off the handle emotionally, or consider it an indictment on our parenting skills, but will see it as confirmation that God's Word is right yet again. In response to their confirmation of God's Word, we will confirm in them His grace and forgiveness for all sins, even those of little hearts.

If you tend to play the 'higher' life form that can never ultimately relate to your child, consider that the Son of God became a lower life form to empathize and suffer with us and for us. The Great Shepherd became a sheep. So we too, as parents, must humble ourselves, stop playing dress up and become, for our children's sake, simple sheep with a shepherd's heart.

* * *

### "Yes, grace but..." - Questions from a Reader

*Q: My husband is a pastor and our two children are teens; one is out of the house and one is still in high school. We did our best to focus on* discipleship, but being the child of a pastor has a lot of pressure from outside the home (and inside too, us being big sinners and all.) I feel like we did our best to disciple them while needing to discipline them for lying, deception, etc. I'm finding it hard to reflect on what you've written here and not feel defensive or think, "This may work for a seven year old, but wait til they hit the teen years! "Our son lied about a relationship he secretly had with an older girl in our church (he was 16, she was 19) and the thing he kept saying over and over was, "I just didn't want to disappoint you." I though we had to be the tough ones and let others (like youth pastors) speak grace into their lives while we raise them. I guess this isn't really a question; I really like what I read in this chapter. I just don't know how to process everything without a lot of guilt, regret, or defensiveness.

I know from my speaking on *House of Grace* at different churches and parenting conferences that my message creates a tension with anyone that has kids in the teen years or that are grown up; there's a natural instinct to measure your performance against what is being presented. And, honestly, that's been one of the scariest things about writing this book. I have a dear friend in ministry that has a prodigal son that, I believe, was triggered or accelerated by authoritarian parenting. It's a secret around the ministry that no one talks about, the disappointing son. Your story and challenges with parenting teens is a common one that I hear a lot. The "I didn't want to disappoint you" reaction is common too, especially in pastors' families. The section you'll definitely want to read is *Chapter 5 -"Becoming an Authority."* It rewires the way we look at and define authority in relationship to our kids, even kids that are teens or have moved to adulthood. I know a number of families with teens that it's helped open communication and reduce the secrecy and increase intimacy between parent and child.

I've traveled a lot doing crisis counseling for pastor-parents and their teens. It's heartbreaking how many congregations put unfair expectations on their pastor and his family, and it's easy to fall unwittingly into that performance trap. Sometimes the kids feel it even when mom and dad aren't even a party to it. Our churches are broken so it makes sense our families are broken too. One of the reasons I felt compelled to write this book now was that I hoped someone would improve on it by the time my daughter is in her teen years; I'm sure I'll need it! And you're right, having other adults to speak grace into their life is important. I love so many youth pastors and youth workers (and not just because they buy our books!)

As for guilt, regret, and defensiveness, it's probably my fault, I wish I would've written a better book, and wait, how is this my fault? Sorry, my sense of humor is inappropriate sometimes. Those emotions are all normal as we process things in hindsight, but I want to encourage you to set them aside for know and forge on with the book. Pray that God reveals truths that you can apply to your teens' lives right this second and, if there is anything you need to confess to them, that God will give you the strength and humility to confess your mess-ups to your teens. I'm going to be writing a book for teens that is sort of a parallel book to House of Grace tentatively titled "*Saying Grace - Improving Your Relationships with Mom, Dad, and Other Frustrating Housemates.*" It's about giving parents and siblings grace, understanding what discipleship is and isn't, teaching how to rebound from sin, rebuilding trust, and, of course, showing empathy to parents who need it too. I'm sorry if I haven't shown enough empathy in this book so far. I pray you see more of it in the pages that follow.

Q: *In your story about the broken cell phone, did the dad make the girl pay him back for the phone?*

Good catch. Let me ask you this, if your neighbor walks into your house, picks up your phone from the kitchen counter, then slams it on the ground shattering it in pieces, what are you going to do? Hopefully not take a swing at him but make him pay for it, right? If he refuses, you'll most likely sue him. To which I reply, "So you want to sue your kid with a similar punitive attitude with a the goal of the offended party (you) being made whole through restitution?" We harp about consequences for our kids but, again, we want to avoid them ourselves. Like one of the big consequences of getting pregnant is kids break your stuff! Can you teach your child how you're going to replace the phone and invite her participation? Of course! That's discipleship and moving through the natural consequences of living life in a time where we must have a phone on us twenty-four hours a day. For grace's sake, treat her more lovingly than a stranger who might do the same thing. In adopting this Gospel-rooted philosophy and tone, you've reinforced that she doesn't have to hide when she messes up and that you are for her, not against her.

"The discipleship of your children all comes down to you becoming an authority in your kids' life. Discipleship hinges on you becoming an authority on the amazing grace of God and how a sinner like you can help a sinner like them understand the depths of God's love for them no matter how disobedient or faithless they seemingly become."

— House of Grace

# 4

# DISCIPLESHIP IN ACTION

*"Example preaches a far more effective sermon than precept."* E.M.
Bounds

**AS SPEAKERS, MY WIFE AND I TRAVEL A LOT**, and when
we travel together we always bring our daughter. That means that as a
toddler she had to quickly learn how to behave in a restaurant, or it
was the drive-thru for us all. We didn't want her running wild in the
place or ruining everyone's meals by the sheer volume of her cries. So
we set about to disciple her in the practice of kindness. After all, it is
kindness that cares about the dining experience of others, not to
mention kindness that cares about the child herself feeling peaceful
and happy instead of trapped in a booth.

So, wanting to treat others the way we wanted to be treated, we decided that while our daughter was young we were not going to take her into a restaurant if we didn't think she could handle it. That meant that we would prepare for success, in those early years, by looking for restaurants where we knew she could get fed promptly and by preparing for any wait time by having other activities that would keep her busy.

Managing kids who are bored and filled with energy can be a daunting task for most of us. But rather than looking at it as a chance for a good meal, we tried to see it as an opportunity for discipleship. Our goal was to teach her kindness, and how we often did this was by way of example, not good examples but bad examples. When we would see other kids who were making a scene we pointed them out to her and explained why that behavior was selfish and unkind to others. Then went on to discuss that the child either wasn't ready to be there, or that the parent had failed to prepare for the event. We didn't blame the child, but put the responsibility on the parent who had the social skills to know this behavior was unkind and the skills to help the child to be better prepared. We'd then ask her what the parent could do differently to help their child or say that it's ok for a child not to be ready for restaurants. It wasn't long before she would start seeing misbehavior and would discern by herself parenting styles that were self-indulgent and setting the child up for failure. She felt like she was in the know, and that made her fully mindful of what kindness looked like and what it didn't. The upside of this approach is not some stealthy way of behavior modification, but teaching her discernment and to be aware of context and her surroundings. But it's worth noting that teaching discernment without grace leads to judgmental people; discernment without grace creates a merciless and un-empathetic child.

As part of her discipleship, on the way to the restaurant I would talk with her and remind her that if she couldn't handle it, no big deal, we could just leave. And that's exactly what would happen. If she were uncontrollable, we would leave before our food came but pay the check anyway. I made sure that she saw me, not as mad, but as matter of fact: "I thought you might not be able to handle this today. We'll just slip out before you get embarrassed. But to be kind to the server and owner, I want to pay for our order and leave him a tip." To her credit, she would recover quickly most of the time, and we wouldn't have to leave, because she knew, from experience, that I would do just what I said; it wasn't an idle threat. But, on those days when she just couldn't control herself, when we got to the car, I would remind her what the Bible says about kindness. I would gently tell her that I believed that eating out and doing anything else in public was a privilege, and that just because I wanted to have lunch there it didn't trump other people's rights to eat in peace. My focus was consoling her rather than lecturing her, because my motivation was discipleship and teaching her how to treat and view other people, not disciplining her because I missed out on my favorite pasta dish.

Let me be clear, this is not the easy route. It takes forethought, pre-event discussions in the car, walking through what challenges she's going to face and what options I have as a parent if a worst-case scenario happens, and it takes an attitude of discipleship. But more than that, it takes time, but the pay-off in the end is more than a well-behaved child, it is a child that is mindful of those around her and understands what it means to think of others, as well as herself. The pay-off is a life lived in discipleship and growth.

## Grace in Saying "Yes," Grace in Saying "No"

The truth is that the discipleship of grace involves huge amounts of time and forethought, and that might be why so many parents opt for the swiftness of discipline over discipleship. But in the long run, swift discipline leads to deeper more difficult problems, especially as the child gets bigger and more able to resist parental control.

Discipline is about muscle memory and involves issues of performance. It all boils down to the dos and the don'ts and removes the whys. Discipleship is all about the whys because it helps our children become more mindful of the Holy Spirit rather than mindlessly following the law. Of course, to a baby that has just learned to pull himself up and reach for a hot pan on the stove, the why is of no importance, but as the toddler matures in his emotional and mental capacity the why becomes very important in teaching faith instead of moralism. Unfortunately, the why takes more time and effort on the parent's part than the law of "no." But fortunately, the investment you make now pays off a hundredfold as they grow and learn to trust the relationship and the love you have built with them.

As humans we are naturally selfish. Whether we realize it or not, we tend to govern our kids out of convenience, comfort, and selfishness. I'm not pointing a finger but making a blanket statement on the nature of sinful man, which we all are. When it comes to enforcing the law of discipline, the parent becomes the judge, jury, and executioner: that's the nature of discipline. And truth be told, that judicial response by the parent is most often based on what the parent is feeling or wanting at the moment. This might sound like an unfair assessment but if you think about it for a while you'll see patterns in your life where you react to your children in the moment through the filter of your schedule, your plans, or your ideas of how they should act. So when the child asks for another orange, the law-based parent who wants the last orange themselves, or who is just tired of the continual asking, might respond with a swift "no." After all, "I'm the parent and I make the rules, and since I feel like saying no, they'll just have to deal with it." But the discipleship of grace takes the time to ask why. Why does she want another orange? Why is it beneficial for her to have one or not to have one? And then the parent responds based on the needs of the child, not the desires of the parent. When that's the perspective, the amount of times the child hears "no" is greatly diminished. After all, if what they are asking for is reasonable, not harmful and I am capable of doing it for them, what is wrong with saying yes? In fact, as a parent attempting to build a house of grace, I am constantly looking for opportunities to say "yes."

Of course saying "no" isn't always bad. In fact, it can be kindness to look for small opportunities to say 'no' to your child when "no" isn't going to be devastating. When Addy was younger and everything she asked for was reasonable, I looked for opportunities to say "no" when it would do the least harm and apply the least emotional impact. I didn't look for opportunities to say "no" in order to make a *big* impact or just to get her attention and so establish myself as king of the house, or even to prepare her for the cruel world, as a lot of parents consider important. I looked for opportunities when "no" was the only option because saying yes was an impossibility. But following every no I offered a "yes." It would go like this, "I'm sorry honey we can't go to Disney World today; it would take us 10 hours to get there and I have to work tomorrow. But I was thinking maybe we could go get ice cream." It wasn't "no" for "no's" sake, but "no" out of necessity followed by a grace-filled "yes." The ice cream wasn't a bribe to get out of the Disney disappointment, but a fun activity where I would actually talk about money, travel, and finances so she could better understand the "no" that she received earlier. It was a "yes" to discipleship. This helped her to learn to trust that we aren't punitive, or harsh in our withholding good from her. In other words, we weren't training her in disappointment with a "no" but allowing her to see that while there are many things she can't have, there is always something that she can; she can rebound. So, we look for opportunities to say "yes."

Hayley tells the story of being in line at the grocery store with our then three year-old daughter who asked if she could have some candy. As she held the candy in her tiny little hand Hayley told her "No honey, not today." At which point she quickly put it back on the shelf and said, "OK Mommy." Because we say "yes" way more than we say "no," she wasn't devastated by this response. The checker was amazed and said she'd never seen a kid that sweet. The reason her reaction was so docile and kind wasn't because she didn't want to get punished, it was because she knew how to rebound from "no." That's because we have taken steps to give her perspective, hope, and a bright side to her life. And because of all of this work, tantrums are never a problem. Because she hears "yes" more than she hears "no", we have built trust in our relationship that she doesn't feel a need to rebel against.

Everything that we do as parents should be with one end goal in mind: to preach the gospel and disciple our little sinners all the way through them becoming big sinners. Again, at risk of belaboring the point, that is why we have to have a sober understanding of the gospel, which insists that there is no one righteous, not even one. Knowing this, we can be sure our kids will fail. That said, by way of example, let's go back to that scenario of a small child who is given the privilege of drinking red juice from a glass. But before handing them the glass, the discipling parent gently reminds the child what the natural consequences of dropping the glass will be. Not what the punishment will be, but what the consequences will be; "if you spill that it will stain our white carpet and I won't be able to get it out." "If you spill you won't get any more juice, because that's the last of it." Or a created consequence like "If you spill that you will have to go back to sippy cups, no more big kid glasses for awhile." Those are the consequences. Of course a punishment might be something like "if you spill that you will get a swat" or "no more TV today if you spill that." And while these threats might focus the child more for a moment, there is a strong possibility that because of their age they will forget not only the threat but also the level of the glass, or even that they are holding a glass. Even for older kids the fear of failure has caused many a free throw to be missed and line forgotten in a play; fear of failure doesn't assure success. But love is a far greater motivator. And empathy allows that love to flow. How many times do we, as adults, forget something we should be doing, get distracted from our task, or make a mess by our absent-mindedness? Remembering that we sometimes get distracted and forget things too allows us to empathize with our children and takes the sting out of their forgetfulness.

In the case of spilt juice, I would like to suggest that there is a far greater lesson at stake here than one on holding a cup level and not messing up nice things, and that is the potential lesson on how we manage the failures, mistakes, and sin in our lives. If your child's reaction to their accident is one of indifference, then they probably need more discipling on the consequences, and should join you in cleaning up the spill and researching what tannins are in red grapes and what can remove them from carpet. If they react with great grief, it's important to make sure they exit it quickly through the gospel of grace and that you not become a party to their shame. These children will already want to fix the situation, so your job is to remind them that their performance (or lack thereof) does not determine your love for them.

Well-meaning parents who want to teach their children responsibility often end up teaching them to reject the grace and forgiveness of God and instead to embrace perfection, deception, obsession, or self-hate. When parents value their stuff over their child's understanding of the gospel, they unwittingly move their children further and further away from the grace meant to save them.

So the bawling and grieving child needs to learn grace and forgiveness. And the cavalier child needs to learn about the fruit of the Spirit, specifically kindness. While the secretive or deceptive child who tries to deny or hide the stain needs to be trained up in confession and faithfulness, and so on. But you don't punish these things into existence, you disciple them. Discipline demands that you write out legislation for every spilled juice scenario, demanding conformity: while discipleship teaches understanding, discernment, and wisdom through love and shared experience.

What we have to understand is that the consequences of our child's disobedience can be the same whether given in grace or in the form of punishment. A few years ago, I was speaking to parents on House of Grace at a church and a father approached me and told me that he had recently discovered that his daughter was using her cell phone to bully another girl. This Christian father was distressed by the nature of her taunts and the deceptiveness of a child he thought he knew better than he apparently did. Her words hurt not only her victim but her own parents as well. As the father was talking to me, I asked him what he was going to do. "Of course we will take away her phone, but beyond that I have no idea what to do," he told me. I agreed with the dad, that having a phone could no longer be a privilege she held, but I told him there were two ways he could go about having the initial conversation. He could show her his anger and shock at what she had done. He could ground her and tell her she'd be "cellphoneless" for the next year of her life, and all that wouldn't be beyond the pale for such a terrible act by a teenage girl.

But this little girl was obviously far from God and needed the training of a believing parent over the punishment of an angry one, if she was going to be drawn into the grace of God. So I then explained to him how the same response looks when it is discipleship instead of punishment. Rather than accuse her, the discipling parent would teach her, and so this is what I said, "Sit your daughter down and tell her that you have found her texts and that you need her to understand something. Tell her that bullying is against the law; if anything happened to this girl she bullied she could be found guilty of a serious crime. Not only that, but that you as her parent would be responsible as well. And because of that, as the one who ultimately is responsible for her and her actions, you need to protect her from potential incarceration by taking away her phone. Explain to her that bullying is illegal and so she can no longer have the thing that is helping her to commit a crime. Talk to her about how you want to help and protect her. Ask her why she was talking to the girl the way she was. Find out her motivation and have empathy for her emotional state. After all, there is something in her that is crying out for help, something in her that led her to choose bullying to soothe her soul, and your job as parent is to find out what that is. And you won't find out what that is by attacking her, denying her emotions, or attempting to punish her for her sins. But you have to make it clear that you love her and that you want to help protect her. In addition, you want to understand why she not only feels this way about the girl but what it is inside her that compels her to punish others. This conversation, rather than being feared, should be considered a discipleship opportunity that God has given you so that you and your daughter can not only grow in love but work together to till the soil for the Holy Spirit to grow his fruit in her life."

Some of the most difficult teaching moments become the most amazing spiritual blessings when you look at them not as a trial to be given and a judgment to be laid down but as insight into the sinful soul of your child and a foray into discussions that will fundamentally alter her life forever. When you get a vivid view of the sinfulness of your child's heart, it is better to lift your hands in praise that God has given you access to her heart than to recoil in disgust. In these moments, consider that you are being given the priceless opportunity of administering God's grace to a child who, now more than ever, understands the need for a Savior and is looking for an answer to the darkness within themselves.

The grace-filled parent knows that they have the opportunity to give their child their second, third, and even fourth chance in life when the rest of the world won't. And in that they have the opportunity to teach them just a fraction of the grace of God. It's the difference between being a police officer and a trusted counselor, a judge and an advocate, a warden and a restorer, between running a penal system and embracing the penal substitution of Christ on the Cross. If Christ sees me spilling red juice on the carpet the consequences don't change but the punishment and stain is removed.

Discipline tidies up, and through punishment sweeps aside the more pressing issues of faith: the salvation of the child, their understanding of the gospel of grace, and how the life of faith affects their daily walk. But discipleship embraces the mess, and sees it as an opportunity to speak the love of God into the life of the little sinner in their midst.

## Discipleship Over Punishment

If our goal is to develop the spiritual muscles and character of our children then we have to rely on the Spirit to help us. When we parent in grace, we no longer rely on punishment but on the power of the gospel through grace to train our child. E.M. Bounds wrote in his classic work *The Necessity of Prayer*, "The very end and purpose of the atoning work of Christ is to create religious character and to make Christian conduct." We see this confirmed by the words in Titus 2:14, which describe Christ as he "*who gave himself for us, that he might redeem us from all iniquity, and purify unto himself a peculiar people, zealous of good works.*" (KJV) From this we can easily see that it isn't our work that makes us pure and changes our character, but His sacrifice. So Christian character is a by-product or reflex coming from Christ's atoning and purifying work, not our works.

Bounds goes on to say that, "in the economy of grace, conduct is the offspring of character. Character is the state of the heart and conduct its outward expression. Character is the root of the tree, conduct, the fruit it bears." In other words, you don't teach conduct in hopes that it develops character or changes the heart, you model, teach, and disciple character and that will encourage changes in conduct and heart.

The trouble comes when we see the end results, character, as our goal. For the believer, the only goal should be to know and love God more. And from that goal comes the offspring of all that is good character.

So how do we go about practically emphasizing discipleship over punishment? It might help if we separate the two this way: punishment is usually reactionary and modifying, while spiritual discipleship is both preparatory and restorative.

First let's take a look at preparation for disobedience, as opposed to reaction to disobedience. The graciousness of preparation is largely overlooked in most families, perhaps because of the forethought and investment of time it requires. But in preparation for potential sin, discipleship walks through scenarios before they have a chance to happen and so arms the child with insight and wisdom that will not only lessen the opportunity for sin, but also help to develop their character and offer a more speedy rebound from sin if they do fall. Our daughter loves going to the dentist, but that is because of the work we put in prior to her first visit, not because of our extraordinary dentist. Knowing how difficult this kind of event could be for a four-year old, we walked her through exactly what would happen. We even acted it out; we played dentist. And this awareness of what to expect not only prepared her but calmed her as she felt in the know, rather than having something sprung on her, leading to surprise or fear. And this same kind of preparation can go into all aspects of life, from teaching them to help out around the house, to preparing them for school, relationships, and work. Preparing them for those events in their lives where their maturity levels might be tested and come up wanting is an act of offering grace and discipleship, and greatly alleviates the need for physical discipline in the future.

Discipleship is also restorative rather than modifying. Both restoration and modification are aimed at the same thing, change. When talking about cars, restoration is concerned with the authenticity, that the components are what the original manufacturer intended, while modifying a car is done purely on the owner's whim and is usually based on appearances. Want to bolt a spoiler on the trunk? Go for it. Don't want to take the time to address a rust issue on the fender? Just paint over it. Restoration and modification both can come after our children sin. Modification is aimed at changing behavior through taking something away, adding a punitive task, or spanking, anything that will force our child to modify their external behavior, while restoration is aimed at deepening an awareness of the gospel of grace. So, restoration doesn't seek to change the behavior of the child in order to change their character. Restoration looks at the heart of the child in order to teach them to apply the gospel to their sin and so to rely on his justification when they fail rather than rely on their own. Because when character change happens, behavior matches the character. But **just modifying behavior is like painting over rust; it looks good for a while until the untreated rust underneath bubbles up and ruins the paint job.** Not only that, but the rust has eaten away at the metal and is worse than before the cosmetic paint job was applied now needing even more radical restoration.

The goal for Christian discipline isn't better conduct, but a stronger understanding of the gospel of grace. As parents we are meant to teach our children who God is and what he has done for us, and because of that all discipline is meant to be spiritual, leading them to a greater understanding of the love of God, not to better our child's conduct in hope that it will result in an understanding of the love of God.

### Forgiveness in Action

God's grace comes with his abundant and unrelenting forgiveness. And so any understanding of this grace must include an understanding of the depths of forgiveness. What we teach our kids about grace at the moment of their failure helps to establish their understanding of the condition of their soul in relationship to their Father. Unforgiven sin requires punishment, and inherently our children understand this. So when we punish them we can easily instill in them a sense of guilt. But our guilt is the object of his grace, the reason for his kindness to us all. And his grace covers not only our mistakes but those of our children as well.

Romans 5:12-21 is a big chunk of scripture but it bears reading at this point. So take a look at this gift of grace:

*"Therefore, just as sin came into the world through one man, and death through sin, and so death spread to all men because all sinned— for sin indeed was in the world before the law was given, but sin is not counted where there is no law. Yet death reigned from Adam to Moses, even over those whose sinning was not like the transgression of Adam, who was a type of the one who was to come. But the free gift is not like the trespass. For if many died through one man's trespass, much more have the grace of God and the free gift by the grace of that one man Jesus Christ abounded for many. And the free gift is not like the result of that one man's sin. For the judgment following one trespass brought condemnation, but the free gift following many trespasses brought*

*justification. For if, because of one man's trespass, death reigned through that one man, much more will those who receive the abundance of grace and the free gift of righteousness reign in life through the one man Jesus Christ. Therefore, as one trespass led to condemnation for all men, so one act of righteousness leads to justification and life for all men. For as by the one man's disobedience the many were made sinners, so by the one man's obedience the many will be made righteous. Now the law came in to increase the trespass, but where sin increased, grace abounded all the more, so that, as sin reigned in death, grace also might reign through righteousness leading to eternal life through Jesus Christ our Lord."*

How can we teach our children about this amazing grace of God without sharing it with them? If we cannot offer the same kind of bold grace in the face of their trespasses, then how can we accept his? It might help to consider this twist, when you are struggling with the sins of your children, realize that they are not sinning against you, but God. And he has already made his position clear: the blood of Christ covers it all. So why then would we exact more punishment than he? (More to come on this in the next chapter, *Becoming an Authority*.)

When we disciple our kids our actions can be similar to those who only discipline, but the narrative and the relationship is much different. Because of that, discipleship requires the commitment of time, energy, and thought. It requires the effort to explain how the gospel relates to the sin in our child's life. This means that, for the discipling parent, unforgiveness is not an option.

## Teaching the Law in Grace

Teaching the law isn't inconsistent with grace, but is consistent with a heart of love and an expectation of failure. When our focus is love instead of performance, our approach to the law focuses on the kindness and mercifulness of God instead of the wrath of God. When we expect failure, not hopefully, but soberly, then we are not tempted to resent their sin, but to see it as proof that none of us can survive without God's saving grace.

So, when we teach, we remind, we don't demand because we relate to the law as sinners ourselves and so we intimately understand and empathize with the state of our child's heart. The subtleness of the word "remind" (as opposed to "demand") shows up in Titus 3:1-3 where Paul says to:

*"Remind them to be submissive to rulers and authorities, to be obedient, to be ready for every good work, to speak evil of no one, to avoid quarreling, to be gentle, and to show perfect courtesy toward all people. For we ourselves were once foolish, disobedient, led astray, slaves to various passions and pleasures, passing our days in malice and envy, hated by others and hating one another."*

This passage is packed with the message of grace as he tells us to "remind" our little disciples of the precepts of God, knowing they will soon forget them as their flesh screams for dominion, but we are not harsh with them because "we ourselves were once" (or often are) just as foolish. This remembering of our own spiritual immaturity is essential in the house of grace.

### Discipleship through Friendship

Most kids consider their best friends the authority on everything in their lives. What their friends think about them shapes their thoughts and their choices. This is one of the reasons why so many young people succumb to peer pressure: they want the acceptance and approval of their friends. They consider them to be experts and go to them with their biggest doubts and concerns. In these relationships they get the comfort and guidance they are looking for, along with acceptance and a sense of being understood. Friendship, especially best-friendship, establishes authority, that's why parents are hyper aware of the dangers of "bad influences," and so eagerly want their kids to have "good" friends.

But for a parent to be their child's best friend is an entirely different thing. For most, friendship between parent and child is considered just as dangerous as friendship with the "bad kid." It's in a different sense, but we do often consider friendship to be a detriment to authority, which I think I've just established isn't the case.

Proverbs 17:17 says that, "A friend loves at all times, and a brother is born for adversity." When adversity hits, don't you want your child coming to you instead of another? Why wouldn't we want our children to consider us the best, most caring, and most reliable person in their lives? The one they go to for all their answers? The best friend they have? Being our child's best of friends doesn't exclude us from being an authority, but can actually develop and expand our authority.

Jesus does not say to us "I am your savior, not your friend" but instead he says, "No longer do I call you servants, for the servant does not know what his master is doing; but I have called you friends, for all that I have heard from my Father I have made known to you" (John 15:15.) In a house of grace, children learn early on that their parents are a source of kindness and not punishment, of teaching and not reaction, of empathy and not judgment and so as they see their parent as a resource rather than an enforcer they find more reasons to come to them for help rather than to run from them and hide.

A discipler is a friend with good judgment, not a judge that discourages friendship. A friend can be honest and offer guidance, but friends don't consider themselves better. A friend relates, empathizes, and loves no matter what. And this reaction to their sin, failure, and shortcomings keeps them coming to us rather than running from us.

The discipleship of your children all comes down to you becoming an authority in your kids' life. Discipleship hinges on you becoming an authority on the amazing grace of God and how a sinner like you can help a sinner like them understand the depths of God's love for them no matter how disobedient or faithless they seemingly become. When you are an expert on grace your kids will come to you as a friend and trusted counselor rather than run to friendship with the world. Your discipleship will become like the air that they breathe; it will be an integral part of their lives for years to come.

\* \* \*

### "Yes, grace but…" - Questions from a Reader

*Q: I've heard many times that my child needs me to be the parent, not a friend. Can you expand on that some more? I'm afraid I'll swing too much to the permissive side of parenting.*

OK, I'm going to make this a bonus section because I probably should've included more on this in the chapter. Can you imagine someone saying to Jesus, "Be their savior, not their friend!"? Of course not. Actually, maybe you can. Jesus, "friend of sinners" was not a compliment the religious experts heaped upon the Son of God.

*The Son of Man came eating and drinking, and they say, 'Look at him! A glutton and a drunkard, a friend of tax collectors and sinners!' Yet wisdom is justified by her deeds." -Matthew 11:19*

It was a "looking-down-their-nose", scoffing judgment. That's how I interpret the well-meaning (and half-right) advice of pastors and parenting experts that say to moms and dads, "be their parent, not their friend."

### Be the parent

This is the half-right portion of the statement. Be responsible for your kids, legally, physically, emotionally, and spiritually. Be responsible. What makes you a parent, and adoptive parents everywhere will testify to this, is not biology, it's responsibility. It's you as a mom or dad standing up and saying, "this child is mine and I'm responsible for her/him. I'm the one person who will love him/her unconditionally until I fail, and then I'll confess my failure and try again." A responsible parent never disowns their child. **Let me say that again. "Being the parent" means that you never disown the child.** If you do, that means that you aren't being the parent. The child may disown you; children do that from time to time, and it hurts. But being the parent means you never disown the child.

Look at, again, the parable of the two sons (the prodigal.) The father never disowns the child, even when the prodigal essentially says, "I wish you were dead" to the father (he wanted his inheritance now.) The father complies and then waits for his son to return. And upon the son's repentant return, there were no lectures or conditions, only a party. The elder son though, what does he do in response to the younger son's return?

### He disowns his brother

*"But he answered his father, 'Look, these many years I have served you, and I never disobeyed your command, yet you never gave me a young goat, that I might celebrate with my friends. But when this son of yours came, who has devoured your property with prostitutes, you killed the fattened calf for him!' And he said to him, 'Son, you are always with me, and all that is mine is yours. It was fitting to celebrate and be glad, for this your brother was dead, and is alive; he was lost, and is found.'" -Luke 15:29-32*

### "This son of yours..."

The "moral" elder brother uses language that distances and disowns his brotherly relationship and puts it ownership squarely on the father. While not right, this happens too; siblings disown siblings. But the father decides to "be the parent" and love unconditionally and offer grace extravagantly.

### "...not their friend."

If "Be the parent" was the half right part of the saying, "...not their friend" is the half wrong (or all wrong) part of the saying. It's well intentioned; I just wanted to point out that this advice is not mean-spirited or harsh. The admonition to de-friend your child is probably a reaction to the perceived permissive parent (and even the neglectful parent.) You know, the mom or dad that's seen as a buddy and not a responsible figure in the child's life. Buying alcohol for their under aged children and their friends is one example that comes to mind. Or the parent that lets their child wear whatever inappropriate clothing they want out of the house. You get the picture.

But before we accept this apparent truism at face value, let's ask what good is a friend? A friend is someone that you can tell your secrets to. A friend is someone who you trust to influence your life and decisions. A friend is someone that shares the same interests (or loves to hear about, support and takes an interest in your interests.) A friend is someone who knows what you're going through because they are going through it too or they have gone through it. Or, at the very least, a friend is willing to try and understand and give you time and support as you're going through it. So defriending your child does not benefit your child. Perhaps it's time we refriend our children in light of the gospel.

"We all need an authority to look to for guidance, and for kids that is especially true in the area of sin. Their bad choices, their suffering, the rejection they experience, all come with questions, and you, whether you believe it or not, are equipped to answer those questions, not because you are highly educated in biblical counseling or child psychology, but because you are an expert in the ways of sin."

– House of Grace

# 5

# BECOMING AN AUTHORITY

*"A child cannot be what they cannot see." David Platt*

SO WHAT DO YOU DO NOW? What do you do if you've taken a look at your life and seen that you have not been the authority in your kid's life? What if you've spent your time living as a permissive parent, or an authoritarian; how do you make the change to authoritative without destroying any chance that you might have of being taken seriously and being respected? Change can feel like waving a white flag and giving up your power to your child. But that's a big fat lie. Change isn't the enemy of love it is the symptom of it. God is in the business of changing you yearly, daily, and hourly. It is only the perfect person that doesn't need change, and there is no perfect person on the planet, so change only signifies a life in the process of being sanctified by the Holy Spirit. Change is meant to be embraced as not only essential to the life of faith but as a sign of salvation. If you aren't changing then you aren't growing and if you aren't growing then you are dying.

### Ask God for Guidance

For change to happen you've got to take a sober look at your parenting life and see those places where you, through misunderstanding, good intentions, or sinful choice, have messed up. Consider the areas in your parenting skills that need work and also consider those areas in your child's life where you see the affects of your parenting style affecting their spiritual life. And the biggest part of this process is prayer. Take your questions to God and spend the time with him and his word to find out where you have been blind, where you need change, and where you have to confess your sins to him. After you make this assessment of the current situation, it's time to get going making the change.

### From Authoritarian to Authoritative

Let me now address the authoritarian parent. If you have been practicing this kind of parenting and you are seeing the holes in your logic, then there will be some dramatic change that will take place. So where do you begin? How do you make such a big change without looking like a hypocrite? The answer lies in the culture of confession that I talked about earlier. Part of loving others and teaching them the reality of the gospel is being free to confess where you have messed up. And without this confession, no parent will create a house of grace.

A couple of years ago, my wife shared this idea of my book *House of Grace* with a friend. This friend was raising two little girls in a family of faith. She loved her kids very much and so quickly saw great value in offering them grace where before she had only offered discipline. At first, when the change came, her girls were surprised. They expected punishment and got a warm embrace and an offer of grace. The mother later commented that she had never had so much peace in the home as when she confessed her lack of grace to her children and promised them that from now on she would offer them the same kind of grace that God had offered her. The result, for her, has been phenomenal. The strife in the house has evaporated, the family is enjoying one another, and the mother's stress level has plummeted, all because she was willing to risk exposing her error in favor of revealing her God.

### From Indulgent or Permissive to Authoritative

The same culture of confession needs to be applied to the indulgent or permissive parenting mistake. If you have been indulging the flesh of your child or failing to disciple them at all, then this awareness is your opportunity to teach them the gospel truth that we are to live by the Spirit, not the flesh. The root of the problem isn't your child and their sin, but a confession of you and your sin, the sin of your parenting motive. It has to be expressed to your child that you have been parenting them with a motive of something other than bringing glory to God. Whether your motive has been your own pleasure in giving them all they want, a drive to make sure they have more than you had, a personal distaste of the law, or just a case of laziness and not working at the difficult task of developing discernment, you can confess your living in the flesh. This sets up the gospel message of the presence of sin in all of our lives. And then leads to the discussion of the blood of Christ covering this sin and giving you a new life.

The indulged child might have a hard time accepting that their "easy" life is ending, but the truth will reach their heart, the heart that longs for a more authentic relationship with their parents, one that isn't based on a disinterest, stuff, and ease, but based on true and involved love. When you commit to act in grace towards your child, you commit to act in favor of the gospel, and that means that all your actions have love for God as their motive, not for self.

## From Neglectful to Authoritative

If you feel that up until now you have been a neglectful parent, let me first say that God is pleased, not in your neglect but in your recognition of the sin in your life. When we see our actions as God sees them, when we fearlessly agree that what he calls sin is indeed sin, it is because our eyes have been opened by the Holy Spirit himself. In these moments when we see our ugliness, when our sin confronts us like a slap in the face, the first reaction is often shame. And that is for a purpose, it is meant to drive us to change. As we see in scripture, "Godly sorrow brings repentance that leads to salvation and leaves no regret, but worldly sorrow brings death" (2 Corinthians 7:10, NIV). But we have to let this godly sorrow do its work, which is to drive us to change, rather than to let it destroy us, to paralyze us, or to depress us.

When you have a neglected child, you have a child that longs for connection but oftentimes doubts things will change. The neglected child needs to both see and hear change in their parent's life. And so a verbal expression of grief is the first step to change. Then after this expression, time and action is needed to confirm the words you have spoken to your child. In order to be more authoritative in their lives, you have to prove yourself to be repentant and in that repentance prove to them that God is actively working in their lives through yours to bring about a change that they so deeply desire.

The confession of your failure might seem like a dangerous thing, but without your confession your child will not see the hand of God actively at work, rather with your confession they will begin to see God's Word living and active in their lives. The enemy would have you hide your sin; swept under the rug. But God wants your sin out in the open where His light can cleanse it. So do not fear coming clean about your failure and openly embracing a new way of relating to your children in the grace of God.

## The Steps to Becoming an Authority

The word authoritative works so well as a descriptor, not just because of the reasons the researchers have mentioned, but also because it describes the discipling parent to a tee. The discipler is an authoritative figure that the child is confident they can approach to learn more about their God and their lives. The discipling parent knows that children are forever growing and learning and naturally look to authority in the areas where they have questions. In fact, we all, whether we are looking to make a life decision or struggling with the trials of our lives, naturally look for counsel, for encouragement, and even sympathy in relationship to authorities on the things we are dealing with. How many times have you yourself searched the Internet looking for authority on the things in life that you have questions about? When making life decisions we all naturally look to authorities on those decisions to counsel us. That's why kids struggle so much with peer pressure, they are continually looking to the lives of their peers to be their authority on being a kid, to guide them through life, and to speak answers into their souls. Whether they look to their friends who are going through the same things, to role models, or to other religions for answers, they know they have to find an authority to help them through life. Children need an authority on the difficult choices, experiences, feelings, and conditions in their lives.

In order for you to become that authority in your child's life, you must reveal expertise they desire through God's wisdom. In order to do that, let's take time to consider what kind of authority your kids are searching for. Most children are not looking for an authority on perfection, being good, or having the law memorized. Most of them aren't sitting in their rooms wishing someone understood their passion for obedience or doing whatever pleases their parents. But most of them are wishing they had someone who got them, who got their weaknesses, who understood their inability to get it right. They are looking for an expert when it comes to embarrassment, rejection, bad choices, and suffering. They are looking for someone who has been there and done that and can relate to them, who can empathize with them and guide them, encourage them and comfort them as they learn how to survive life as an imperfect human being.

To do this, you have to start talking with your child about yourself, not in order to impress them with how good a person you are, but to reveal to them how much you are alike. They have the same DNA as you, so I know they are a lot like you (even if they are yours through adoption, they still share the same sinful spiritual DNA from our first parents and are still sinners within reach of God's grace) and this realization will signal the beginning of a changed relationship. *The camaraderie of grace is the foundation of all your authority in their life.*

Just as I said in the first chapter of this book, confession teaches the necessity of the gospel as it embraces the truth about our sinful hearts as well as the grace of our God. You know your kids and where they stand spiritually, so these conversations have to be built around raising your child in the way that they should go, but the first step has got to be an apology. You have to first apologize for failing to live out the gospel in their lives. And this has to also then, be accompanied by the presentation of the gospel, not like a book report, but in a heartfelt explanation of what the gospel has done in your life.

And if you say, "But I've already confessed my sins, I've already given them the gospel," let me just remind you that confession isn't a one time event in the life of faith, and it isn't going to be a one time event in the life of your child, but this initial confession that represents a change in the way you parent is crucial for their understanding of the gospel of grace. We have raised our daughter in this kind of household her entire life, but there are still days when we, overcome by the depth and rawness of our sin nature, have to make this confession all over again. It's like saying "I love you," it isn't a one-time event and it never gets old. And as they are repeatedly exposed to this amazing grace that you relate to them and offer them, it begins to imprint on their soul and to feed their desire to share this same stuff with others.

### Disciple your Child

Next, you need to let them know that God has revealed to you the areas where he wants change in your relationship. Let them know how much you love them and explain to them that you are going to start to show that love the way God has shown his love to you. You can explain that you aren't throwing out the truth of the law but that you are going to treat the law as it was meant to be treated; evidence of our sinfulness and God's holiness. And explain to them the difference between God's law and your own. It is crucial for your kids to understand what the law is meant to do, and how we as humans tend to use the law to get what we want, in this case, obedience, peace, or respect.

### You Don't Have to Be On the Same Page

The way that a house of grace works best is when the whole house serves grace. So it is good to have these conversations with your spouse so that you can get on the same page, but it isn't essential. If your spouse refuses to embrace the idea of grace, that doesn't mean that you are forced to do the same. This grace we share with others isn't optional, but a requirement on the believer, so even if you don't see the same grace in your spouse you can still offer it. We see this in

# BECOMING AN AUTHORITY

1 Peter 3:1-2 when it comes to the case of a believing spouse living with an unbelieving spouse, "*Likewise, wives, be subject to your own husbands, so that even if some do not obey the word, they may be won without a word by the conduct of their wives, when they see your respectful and pure conduct.*"

**Again, Pray**

Once you know God wants you to do something, to make some kind of change, you might feel completely unequipped to do it, but the fact that God has ordained it gives you all the power you need. But to call on that power, you have to call on God by way of prayer. Ask him daily for guidance, wisdom, and the faith to trust in his grace over your performance, and your kids' performance.

\* \* \*

When it comes to parenting, the best the world can do is tell you that you have to find a balance between authoritarian and permissive parenting, but the gospel reveals something much better. Unlike the world that speaks like Mr. Miyagi in *The Karate Kid*, "balance is key," the gospel reveals a huge imbalance. There is nothing balanced about an all-powerful holy God that the world sees as an authoritarian, sacrificing his son for all of mankind. That is wholly imbalanced. It wasn't just enough blood spilled to cover all of mans' sins, it was wholly, far too much, more than enough for all of mankind. When we as believers approach parenting with the goal of balance in mind, we abandon the gospel in favor of man-made scales of justice and fairness. Scales coincidently held by lady justice in front of every courthouse in the country, which again leads to us falling back on the law as our primary parenting tool instead of the gospel of grace. Now let's look at the specific areas of life where our kids need an authority to live in the center of that grace.

138

## An Authority on Sin

Whenever we find the need to discipline our children it is because we want to curb the sin or failure in their lives. At the heart of it, most of us understand the need to eradicate sin, to point it out and to teach our kids to avoid it. The trouble is that when we set ourselves up as experts on the law instead of experts on sin, we end up looking like hypocrites in our children's eyes. That's why the authoritative parent has to be first and foremost an authority on sin, meaning that you know sin intimately because you sin every single day. The gospel then becomes a part of your everyday conversation, "I sinned today, and I'll sin tomorrow. I don't have the power to be perfect, but Christ is my perfection, and he is yours." Since Romans 3:23 tells us that our children are also sinners, "for all have sinned and fallen short of the glory of God," they need an expert sinner to turn to when dealing with the struggles in their lives. And that expert is meant to be you. But when you fail to expose your own sinful heart, to confess your sin and to speak the truth of God's Word that everyone is sinful, you end up confusing your sinful child. Your insistence that the law is doable, that you are a good example of how easy it is, only alienates you from them, and sends them looking to other sinners like themselves for advice on what it means to be a sinner. The gospel of grace seems dangerous to most parents because it forces them to articulate to their kids, "because of our sin nature, it's normal to make mistakes, normal to fall, normal to fail, normal to be less than perfect." It seems counter-intuitive to articulate inevitable failure. So we parent with a white-knuckled grip on the law and preach perfection while we save grace for special occasions. But saving grace isn't Saving Grace. Wouldn't you much rather be the expert sinner in your child's life so that you can point them to the saving work of Christ, instead of encouraging them to run to another little sinner who, finding no hope in the gospel, points them in the direction of embracing their sinful hearts? Wouldn't you rather be the expert they run to?

The only way you can be the one your child turns to for the problem of sin, both their own and that which is inflicted on them, is if you are honest with them about the power of sin and the power of grace in your own life. Natural performance-based parenting for the believer is usually focused on how not to sin. But spiritual parenting, seeing parenting as discipleship, is focused on conversations about why we sin, the root cause of sin, and how to bounce back from sin. Instead of simply focusing on avoiding sin, or covering it up, the authoritative sinner gets honest about the human condition and fearlessly groups themselves together with their child in a human category, rather than a god category; parent and child both sinful from birth (see Psalm 51:5). This not only gives your child freedom from the chains of performance but it also frees you at the same time from building your reputation on the performance of your kids.

A few years ago some friends of ours were having trouble dealing with the sin in their teen's life. He was a good Christian boy, star athlete, leading in the youth group, the "perfect" child. So when the parents found inappropriate texts on his phone between him and his girlfriend (also in the youth group) they were in disbelief. They called my wife and I for counsel and we sat down to help them figure out next steps. "How could this be? What did we do wrong?" they asked us. Their first reaction was filled with surprise, they didn't see it coming and so they were grief stricken and furious all at the same time. And they were embarrassed because they were going to have to tell the girl's parents and out their son as "not as honorable" as they had represented when he first asked to date their daughter.

"How could he do this to us?!" was the next question. I calmly answered them, "I didn't read the texts, but I'm pretty sure the "doing" didn't involve you." My attempt at levity was also an attempt to move them away from the god category (that they were sinned against) and over to the human category (all sinners.) I refocused them off of "why did he do this?" It's called hormones, puppy love, and sin. Instead, reminded them of their shared history in this area when they were young (I knew their testimonies) and I wanted them to think about and ask the question of themselves and their son, "why is this something you would hide? If you believe this is good and allowable in your life, why not be a man (albeit a young one) and stand up for what you believe?" And lastly, "do you understand the dangers of a double life; saying you believe one thing and acting another way in private?" Instead of shaming their son toe-to-toe in their embarrassment, they walked side-by-side in revealing to their son what they had found and how he was going to step up and rectify it with his girlfriend's parents. Then they needed to say to their son, "which way do you want to live? We will love you no matter what, but please don't lead a double life." This event turned out to be a bonding one for the young man and his parents; he knows that they are authoritative on sin and secrets, and that they'll lovingly restore him in spite of their potential for experiencing "embarrassment" over raising a sinner.

In natural parenting, the law exists to produce a certain type of adult, to produce the most preferable outcome. In spiritual parenting however, with the gospel as its foundation, the law exists to reveal our spiritual condition and our need for a savior, not to measure our performance. The reality is that the law's existence gives each and everyone of us a failing grade. And we receive this grade the moment we exit the womb. So the illusion that our child can maintain a perfect moral GPA with enough blood, sweat, and tears - some the parent's, some the child's - is a lifelong exercise in futility.

The way to teach your child to grow, to learn from their mistakes and to embrace the love and grace of God is to not be surprised when they sin, to not be angry, disappointed, or to take it personally, but to be sober in your understanding of sin's power and presence in the lives of us all. We are not to be unaware in life and taken by surprise when humans that we love and want to protect prove God's Word to be true. You are not perfect and to expect your child to be is to call God a liar. But when you fearlessly group yourself together with your child, admitting your human condition, then you prepare yourself and your child to embrace the full grace of God.

We all need an authority to look to for guidance, and for kids that is especially true in the area of sin. Their bad choices, their suffering, the rejection they experience, all come with questions, and you, whether you believe it or not, are equipped to answer those questions, not because you are highly educated in biblical counseling or child psychology, but because you are an expert in the ways of sin.

There was a time when our daughter adopted the exasperating phrase, "okay, okay, OKAY!" whenever we asked her to stop what she was doing on her iPad or computer and to do what we wanted her to do. After a couple weeks of that phrase frequenting her speech, in order to get her attention, my wife told her that she would need to punish her. Hayley told her she was going to talk to me about what punishment she deserved and left the room. When Hayley talked to me about it I quickly reminded her that we don't punish, we disciple, and then I coached her on what to say. Hayley returned to her and did just what I had suggested, and here is their conversation. "I am sorry Honey. I know that you were impatient with me just as I am often impatient with you. And that is because we are all sinners; we all struggle with selfishness and wanting things to go the way we want them and then we get exasperated when they don't. And I'm sorry that I said I would punish you because we don't believe in punishing but in discipling you. So let's talk about what it is in you that makes you talk like that to me. And not because I am trying to make my life easier but because I don't want you to talk to others like that and ruin friendships or to be seen as a bratty child by your friend's parents, or to be thought poorly of as a follower of Christ. So I notice that you talk to me in that way when I ask you to stop using your devices. Do you think that's true? "Yes," she said, "but not just then, sometimes I do it when you ask me to brush my teeth."

As Hayley smiled at this additional confession she said, "You're right. But I find that when you talk with your friend on FaceTime you are more prone to start talking that way to me. Does she talk like that to her parents?" "Yes," she said, "and to her sister." "Okay, well why don't we try this. Since I don't want you to stop being friends with her, and I know she is just a child and will grow and learn to control her emotions over time, let's do this. Since you are usually frustrated with me after you FaceTime, let's say no devices after you FaceTime your friend. That way we can try to help you look at why you copy the bad behavior of your friend and try to look at her behavior through the filter of Christ. And that way we won't have to fight."

When she heard this my daughter cheerfully said, "Sure! That sounds good." And they proceeded to have a wonderful and joyful bedtime. Thank God that we don't take the easy route of punishment instead of taking the time to discipling her through it! The tone would have been much more combative and less educational if we would have put punishment over discipleship.

Your child is continually looking for an authority on life and if it isn't you then it is going to be somebody. So when it comes to the sin in their lives, if you pretend to have no idea why they sin the way they do then guess what, they will find someone who does seem to understand them and seek them out for guidance and advice. But if you are willing to be transparent with your own life and to offer yourself not as an authoritarian who simply enforces the law, but as an authority who understands the sinful heart, then you will find yourself to be the go-to person when the trials of life come.

### An Authority on Bad Choices

A lot of us struggle with how much of our sin to share with our kids, especially in the area of sexual purity. The thought of your sin giving them permission to do the same things you did or of losing your authority by appearing sinful can lead to secret keeping about your past and a focus on only the stuff you've done right. But telling them only the things you've done right makes you an authority on perfection and the law, not on grace. And as an authority on the law you become like a police car that's mere presence causes drivers to slow down, but once you are out of sight, it's pedal to the metal. The ironic truth is that when you are an authority on bad choices you become an authority on good choices.

So how do you become an authority on bad choices without giving your kids a green light to do all that you've done in your life? The answer to that will require some soul searching and discernment. What you have to do is to take an account of your bad choices, what they were, how they affected you, and what you learned from them. The truth is that God uses even your bad choices to perfect you, that's why he says, he works all things together for the good of those who love him. So to try to dissuade your child from bad choices by telling them how much they ruined your life doesn't always work. Especially if they see your life as un-ruined. But being honest about your choices, how they hurt and then how God used them to grow you and draw you near gives those bad choices less power and reveals the power in the grace of God.

Exposing your bad choices is an integral part of your testimony. And those choices, after they have been redeemed and used for the glory of God, are a great way to share the gospel with others. That means for all of us whether parent, friend, or pastor, being honest about our past is essential. When attending a church, one of the quickest ways to know if it is a gospel-centered church is by listening for confessions of the pastor. If he is willing to share his bad choices, to confess them without whitewashing them, and to use them to teach his congregation about the grace of God, then the gospel is being taught by example through a sheep with a shepherd's heart. The same must be true for a home built on the gospel. The depth of sin we have been saved from has to be revealed and your bad choices are a part of that revelation. Being an authority on bad choices allows you to build a house of grace. So don't be afraid to share your past with your children when it is age appropriate.

My wife and I always council others to reveal the bad choices of their past once they have seen the redemption that God has given them and their children are old enough to understand and process their personal history, at least in the way they present it. For instance, if you were divorced before you had your child with your new spouse, you may find yourself sharing this fact with them multiple times over the course of his or her life, starting with the simple explanation when she is little, with much more detail in the tween and teen years. Once those bad choices have proved His faithfulness, then they are prime fodder for the gospel presentation. But, if you are in the throws of your sin, if you are holding on for dear life to your bad choices, using your child as a counselor to confess to is almost always a bad idea. You still need to be confessing your sin, but you need to seek someone with the spiritual maturity to restore you and walk with you in repentance. That job should rarely be for your child.

But you can become an authority on bad choices as soon as you reject your bad choices, by confession and repentance, and embrace God's forgiveness and grace. As you do, you will begin to see what God will make of your failure and then you can share that with the rest of the world. This lesson is a crucial one in the life of a discipling parent because, until you learn it, you cannot truly teach it to your child. I encourage you to spend some time seeking God for insight on the sin in your life and seeking his word for answers. Reading Romans chapters 7 and 8 is a great place to start to better understand the power of the gospel in your rejection of sin.

## An Authority on Guilt

Have you ever called yourself a bad parent? I think everyone has at some point, if only under your breath. But there is a fad growing right now and that is the vocal acceptance of our parenting failure. "Bad Mommy" blogs are popping up all over the news, as some women confess their failure and, in fact, accept them as part of their sinful nature. This idea allows a lot of parents to breathe a sigh of relief for being able to call the guilt they feel bad guilt, not meant for conviction but destruction. This idea of bad guilt is a valid one; bad guilt is thoroughly bad because it takes the topic off of God and puts it firmly on us. Whenever we change the subject to ourselves to the point that it either makes us question God's Word or fear His presence then guilt is bad.

Unfortunately, in the war against bad guilt, good guilt is often collateral damage. In fact, in the war on guilt a lot of people end up believing there is no such thing as good guilt. But it is important for students of grace to first understand the value of guilt, because without our guilt we wouldn't receive the grace of God. In fact, our guilt is the very reason for Christ's coming to earth at all, therefore it ought not be demonized along with bad guilt.

But relying on the extremely important verse from Romans 8:1, "There is therefore now no condemnation for those who are in Christ Jesus"; many misconstrue the purpose of guilt. But God's grace allows for good guilt, in fact it thrives on good guilt. Good guilt is the fertilizer that makes the garden of grace grow. For Godly grief [guilt] brings sorrow that leads to repentance (see 2 Cor. 7:10). Guilt is meant to be the catalyst for driving us closer to God because when a believer finds sin in their lives they are sickened by their rejection of God and want nothing more than to change, to run as far away as they can from sin. The importance of repentance shouldn't be missed as we apply grace to all of our guilt.

Grace is the result of our confession of real sin from good guilt. And here is where bad guilt becomes a valuable concept to understand. Bad guilt is what we feel for doing something that was not against God's Word but against our flesh, against societal norms, or against our own man-made law. Bad guilt is what we feel when we are embarrassed; this usually follows on the heels of humiliation, of not impressing others.

Bad guilt is also what we feel when we have actually sinned against God, confessed that sin, and then decided that we are still not forgiven and so we hold onto self-condemnation. This makes the guilt bad because in our "guilt" we accuse God of lying to us when he says he will freely forgive us all of our sins (see 1 John 1:9). Bad guilt is anything that takes us away from our relationship with God. And there is no grace for this kind of guilt, not until we confess the bad guilt, as the sin of distrust, unbelief, or worry.

Christ died to save us from the condemnation we are under when we transgress God's law, not for the humiliation we feel when we do something we wish we would have done better, or when we fail to impress the Joneses. If we want to build a house of grace we've got to reject our bad guilt, but embrace the idea of good guilt being the stuff that leads us to repentance, to turning away from the sin in our lives.

Many people take the terrific advice of preaching the gospel to yourself everyday and change it into "give yourself grace" everyday. But you are not the source of grace. You don't have the ability, the reserves, or the holiness to give the depths of grace that you need. What you do have the ability to do is to share God's grace with others.

Unfortunately, when we lump all guilt together and call it bad we begin to apply God's grace to ourselves without the act of repentance. In determining that all guilt is bad, we refuse to allow any of it to work the change in our lives that it was meant to work. When we make fun of our guilt, even our bad guilt, we begin to redefine guilt's purpose and in the process we inadvertently begin to embrace our sinful behavior. Rejecting good guilt requires giving yourself grace, which comes from the flesh. But when you receive God's grace it comes from the Spirit.

So is guilt to be your constant companion? Of course not! The more momentary godly grief is, the more quickly it gives way to repentance, the healthier your spiritual walk becomes. But the elimination of any occurrence of godly guilt is a red flag towards a grace glutton self-centered life. And when you look at grace this way, you not only cheapen grace but you distort it to mean acceptance of your sinful behavior. If you see all guilt as bad, then you don't allow guilt to lead to any change; you reject the need for grace on the grounds that your guilt was bad to begin with.

God's law produces godly guilt, but grace has a role in producing guilt as well. If it weren't for the divine light of grace revealing sin in your life then your sinful heart couldn't even grasp the depth of God's love. So his grace comes and enlightens your heart and mind to good guilt, to godly sorrow. Grace precedes and generates Godly guilt. Godly guilt then produces repentance.

Guilt exposes you to godly grief so that you will repent, so that when you fall short again (because there is no one righteous), grace is still there to say, "It's okay, I've caught you." Not like a cop that tackles a suspect, but like a fireman after you've jumped out of a burning house; a fire that your heart set. Grace is not only the arms that you jump into but it is also God's holy sight that he gives you to look around and say "Whoa, I'm in a burning building!" That's godly guilt. Now, conversely, bad guilt never comes from grace, but from fatalism, condemnation, and death. The guilt of grace comes from God and is God-centered, and has a gospel purpose.

When you feel guilt, get down on your knees and seek him and ask through the power of the gospel and his grace, "Is this something that I need to repent of, and does my repenting of it help or hinder the gospel?" What position in your heart does this thing have? Divine the source of your guilt through scripture; is it the Holy Spirit convicting you or is it the world? When your child is wrestling with guilt, help her discern whether it's good guilt or bad guilt; if it's good, lead her to repentance and grace. If it's bad guilt, free them from the chains of unnecessary performance, people pleasing, poor boundary setting, or whatever else might be heaping guilt on their precious heart.

## An Authority on Suffering

Suffering happens, there is no getting away from it. It happens to you and it will happen to your kids. Suffering can come cruelly from both cancer cells and a mean girl's texts. And it's all spiritually pointless, if not destructive, if you look at it as a curse, plague, or regret. But if you can look at it in the right spiritual light, suffering can serve the sufferer by giving them empathy, compassion, perseverance, character, and wisdom (see Romans 5:3-4; 2 Cor. 1:4; James 1:2-4). But that's not the natural outcome of suffering. A natural view of suffering sees no good purpose in it. And while not usually caused by sin, suffering only serves its spiritual purpose if we allow it to put an end to our natural focus on ourselves and, instead, focus more on our Savior.

Severe physical afflictions aside, it can be easy as a parent to look on your kids' daily suffering and their complaint as melodramatic, childish, and selfish. We can see their writhing in the pain of a splinter as unacceptable and we can easily determine that we have to teach them to get over it quickly and to toughen up. And while both of these things may be true, how we go about teaching these lessons either applies the grace that God gives to us in our suffering or infers upon him an uncaring and harsh-handed reaction to the human condition.

Since you know that your kids are going to suffer, both physically and emotionally, being an expert on the topic is an important part of discipling them. But being an expert on suffering isn't just about having suffered but about what that suffering has taught you.

### EMPATHY

And for anyone who wants to disciple another, suffering is meant to teach the very important lesson of empathy, the ability to put yourself in the shoes of another who is suffering. Empathy is an important tool in your discipling toolbox. As we read in 2 Corinthians 1:4, the God of Comfort, "comforts us in all our affliction, so that we may be able to comfort those who are in any affliction, with the comfort with which we ourselves are comforted by God."

Empathy is one of the most essential traits for a grace-filled parent, but especially in becoming an authority on suffering. But unfortunately is an often misunderstood and missing trait in a parent's life. The farther we get from our own childhood the more difficult it comes to put ourselves in the shoes of our children and to remember how we felt as we experienced many of the same things as they. But empathy doesn't need a strong emotional memory in order to exist. To help you with the concept of empathy let me first talk about the difference between empathy and sympathy. Sympathy feels pity for others; it feels bad for them. But unlike empathy it doesn't understand the feeling. And so sympathy can oftentimes lead us to say things that search for a silver lining but don't relate to how a child is feeling. Like if your child is suffering because they got picked last when their friends were splitting up into teams and you say, "Well, at least you got picked." Sympathy attempts to see the good in spite of the suffering the person is experiencing. But empathy "gets" the feeling, though you may not have experienced the exact feeling, you still have empathy because you can allow them the feeling, having experienced your own suffering. Empathy might say to the same child, "I know it's hard getting picked last. I remember one time when I tried out for basketball, I felt like . . . How does it make you feel?" Or even more simply, "I'm so sorry. I'm here." Empathy doesn't try to fix things by telling kids to stop feeling what they are feeling, but it relates to the suffering that happens as you live as a child (and as an adult) without full control of your own life. When you empathize with your children you offer them grace rather than ridicule, criticism, micromanagement, or punishment. You put yourself down as an expert on suffering rather than the inflictor of that suffering and you build a bond with them that they will remember when something really bad happens in their life.

### COMPASSION

After we learn empathy for the sufferings of others, the next step to becoming an authority on suffering is compassion. Empathy understands while compassion is that understanding in action. When we show compassion we effectively offer mercy to our children. And so when they suffer we don't say things like, "that serves you right," or "let this teach you a lesson," but we offer them mercy and share compassion with them by not only understanding their pain but helping them to learn to alleviate it. When our daughter was young and pain was an everyday emotional, and sometimes physical, occurrence, I spent a lot of my time showing her mercy, sometimes by just hugging and comfort, and other times through humor and distraction. The former is obvious; the latter might need an example. So when she would crash into the corner of the table while learning to walk, sometimes I would create a distraction that would get her mind off of her pain. As she got older, I might imitate the same head banging on myself, so she saw me experiencing the same pain and fate. Many times this would produce a strange mix of cries and laughter, but then I would console her while showing her I too was an authority on accidental infliction of pain on myself. Now, years later, I have noticed that she had not only learned to process her suffering with hope, but that she had learned to do the same thing for her hurting friends. And so whenever she saw a child in distress she would quickly console and empathize with the child and sometimes use physical humor that would bond with the child and communicate compassionately that he was not alone.

Many parents that already realize the value of suffering choose to ignore the pain and suffering of their children and instead opt to let them cry it out or say in a detached way, "they'll get over it." But this kind of reaction to the sufferings of others lacks compassion and grace and instead teaches our children that life is cruel and they need to work it out alone. But the mercy of the Father has shown us it is meant to be our example. His mercies never cease; in fact they are new every morning (see Lamentations 3:23). He doesn't withhold his compassion from us to teach us how to comfort ourselves, but is "the God of all comfort" as we learn in 2 Corinthians 1:3. Why would we then, when we wish to teach our children the very nature of God, refuse to comfort our kids when they suffer, even while believing that suffering will be of great value to them?

### PERSEVERANCE

As one who has suffered you have been put to the test, and if you have learned from that suffering then you have persevered. And it is this perseverance, or patience, that is meant to be useful in discipling your child. As you persevere through the trials of parenthood you give your child a visual example of the power of suffering and how much it can benefit a person who is rightly related to Jesus. Being an expert on suffering and the perseverance it teaches is meant to help you relate to your child and help you offer them grace rather than frustration or even anger. As an expert on suffering you have grown and learned to wield grace to your fellow sufferers. Oswald Chambers once wrote:

*"Perseverance means more than endurance– more than simply holding on until the end. A saint's life is in the hands of God like a bow and arrow in the hands of an archer. God is aiming at something the saint cannot see, but our Lord continues to stretch and strain, and every once in a while the saint says, "I can't take any more." Yet God pays no attention; He goes on stretching until His purpose is in sight, and then He lets the arrow fly. Entrust yourself to God's hands. Is there something in your life for which you need perseverance right now? Maintain your intimate relationship with Jesus Christ through the perseverance of faith. Proclaim as Job did, "Though He slay me, yet will I trust Him" (Job 13:15).*

*Faith is not some weak and pitiful emotion, but is strong and vigorous confidence built on the fact that God is holy love. And even though you cannot see Him right now and cannot understand what He is doing, you know Him. Disaster occurs in your life when you lack the mental composure that comes from establishing yourself on the eternal truth that God is holy love. Faith is the supreme effort of your life– throwing yourself with abandon and total confidence upon God."*[ix]

Without suffering in our lives and the lives of our kids, there is no way that we can receive the great gift that is the opportunity to throw ourselves, in faith, "with abandon and total confidence upon God." But let us not confuse our role in this; God is the archer, not us. We must empathize with our children as fellow arrows; we've just flown farther than they have by God's grace.

## The Value of Suffering

In order to teach our kids to suffer well, we have to learn and to share with our children, by way of example, the value of suffering. It's so easy to complain when trials come, to pull and tug to attempt to get out from under them, but this notion of resistance only empowers sin and more suffering. But what God means the suffering to do isn't to destroy us but to perfect us. James 1:2-4 explains with these words, "Count it all joy, my brothers, when you meet trials of various kinds, for you know that the testing of your faith produces steadfastness. And let steadfastness have its full effect, that you may be perfect and complete, lacking in nothing." Teaching our kids this lesson is a part of the lesson for us too. As we count it all joy we must realize that even the struggles we face as parents is a part of this joy making process. The trials a parent may face are meant to perfect not to destroy, and as you see this process coming to life in your family you can begin to turn from complaint to joy and, in so doing, instill this same shift in the mind of your child.

As your child grows in faith they will begin to understand the truths of scripture and find hope in these same words in James that you have found. Small children may be unable to fully grasp the notion through a Bible reading, but will more easily embrace it after years of seeing it manifested in your daily interactions with them. In a house of grace, a parent is a noticer more than a judge. They notice things and serve as a compass that points their child back in the right direction. So when you notice complaint, the grace-filled response isn't judgment on that complaint, because in that you condemn yourself as well, as we read in Romans 2:1, "in passing judgment on another you condemn yourself, because you, the judge, practice the very same things." But a more grace-filled response would be, "I've noticed that you are having trouble with complaining today, and when you complain you have a bad day because you are focusing on the negative. I have days like that too. Is there a specific situation behind all the complaint or is it just 'one of those days'? Sometimes when I'm having one of those days, I try and think about what I can control that would make today better. I would love to help you if I can. But even if I can't help, I'm still here and I still love you."

When you parent without grace, you focus on yourself. You parent based on what you want to put up with, rather than based on what God wants to accomplish in your and your child's life. Parenting in grace opens not only your child's life up to the amazing grace of God, but it also opens up your own and refines you with the suffering associated with the trials of parenting, making them more joyful than painful, and more life changing than life destroying.

## Their Suffering

### WHINING

Most of the time when our kids suffer, we hear about it. They don't suffer well in silence, especially when they are in the safety of their own family. And for a lot of parents, complaint can be a thorn in the flesh, a burr under the saddle of life. And because of that it is natural to snap at complaint and even punish it in order to stop it. But when we focus on ourselves and on how their behavior makes us feel, we make life all about us and forget the spiritual sickness that is behind their emotion. When a parent reacts based on what they don't want to put up with, then they miss a discipleship opportunity in favor of their own comfort. But the prescription for complaint is found in God's Word when he tells us to do everything without complaining (see Phillipians 2:14). So how do you disciple your child and help them to change their vocabulary when it comes to complaint?

## IMITATION

The first thing is to understand that your kids get most of their behavior and communication style from you or whomever they spend most of their day with. What they see in you they imitate. So if they hear a steady monologue of complaint coming from you then guess what will be their speech pattern? Complaint. Complaint comes so natural to the human heart that a lot of the time we are completely unaware of it in ourselves. But think about how many times you have something negative to say about the weather, your health, your co-workers, friends, family members, the restaurant, the check out person, the driver in front of you. Complaint bothers us when it comes out of the mouth of a whiney child, but yet we whine to our Father all day long and barely notice it (but our children do!)

In order to disciple the complaint out of your child, you have to take a sober look at your own topics of conversation. Not only what you say out-loud but what you think about in the quiet of your own heart, because even your thoughts find their way into imitation by little ones who are constantly keeping an eye on you.

## COMPLAINT

So what is the prescription for you and your child? How do you curb a tongue, or mind, that wants to accuse God of not doing his job? The first and most important step is to create a home of thanksgiving. And this doesn't mean that you pull out all the stops each November and spend one day a year thanking God for all he has done. It means making your home a place where thanks is given more than complaint is muttered. You must remind yourself and teach your kids the gospel message, in which we have been forgiven of more than we could ever deserve and because of that, complaint should be the farthest thing from our mouths.

Most self-aware parents will notice that much of the complaint that their kids hear revolves around them and their failure. Complaint, criticism, and accusation are the most common reactions to an imperfect world even to our imperfect children. But our complaint doesn't show our kids the nature of God, who has more to complain about in us than we do in our kids. Yet, the gospel removes the need for complaint and accusation, and makes the believer acceptable in His eyes no matter how deep the sin. When the gospel message is at the heart of a house of grace it becomes the foundation for giving thanks over complaint.

I once listened to a mother recount their recent family vacation. They had gone to a tropical location and stayed in a hotel on the beach. The story, rather than a celebration of time away with the family, was a laundry list of all the things wrong with this hotel. For about twenty minutes she went on about how horrible things were and as she did her son chimed in mimicking her complaint. The sad part is that the things he complained about were not things a normal boy his age would ever complain about; he probably wouldn't have even noticed if she had not made a big deal about them. If she had turned her complaint into praise, if she had practiced a heart of thanksgiving and at least measured all the positive against the "struggles" of their beach vacation, and refused to complain against this gift from God, how differently would her son have responded, and how much more enjoyable would their family vacation have been?

As believers we can't let the trials of our life fuel our complaint muscle or we end up accusing the Provider, and instead teach our kids that God isn't fair, just, or good, as we reject the words, "give thanks in all circumstances" (1 Thessalonians 5:18).

## WORRY

Suffering, or the fear of potential suffering, leads to worry. And worry can be a natural part of childhood as well as parenthood. So being an expert on worry shouldn't be difficult for us. Our expertise isn't the result of continual worry, but our ability to say, "I used to worry like you." It's expertise found on the other side of the debilitating sin of worry.

When we worry over our kids we aren't experts on worry, but slaves to it. And our worry doesn't teach them grace, but law, the law that serves our fear for their safety, "don't do this, stay away from that, that is too dangerous." You cannot be an expert on worry while you are worrying. An expert on sin, no matter what kind it is, is most effectively one who has gotten freedom from that particular sin. Not that they have completely overcome it, but that we have had victory to a significant degree over a significant period of time.

Thinking that our worry for our kids only proves our love for them is self-deception. It does no such thing, because perfect love drives out fear (remember 1 John 4:18?). It doesn't worry over what God will do to us or to those we love. Any action that is motivated by worry is not love but an attempt to protect ourselves from the sovereignty of God. But when you become an authority on suffering you claim the sovereignty of God in all of life's trials, so worry is no longer necessary.

## SICKNESS AND DISEASE

There is no more helpless feeling than that of a parent at a sick child's bedside. The illnesses that my daughter has suffered from pale in comparison to those of precious friends I know. So instead of expanding what I've already written in this chapter with specifics for these situations, let me provide something infinitely more valuable; scripture for all who suffer or are walking with someone who is suffering emotionally or physically.

Deuteronomy 31:6 " ...Be strong and courageous. Do not fear or be in dread of them, for it is the Lord your God who goes with you. He will not leave you or forsake you."

Psalms 138:3 On the day I called, you answered me; my strength of soul you increased.

Proverbs 3:5-6 Trust in the LORD with all your heart, and do not lean on your own understanding. In all your ways acknowledge him, and he will make straight your paths.

Matthew 11:28-29 Come to me, all who labor and are heavy laden, and I will give you rest. Take my yoke upon you, and learn from me, for I am gentle and lowly in heart, and you will find rest for your souls.

2 Corinthians 1:3-4 Blessed be the God and Father of our Lord Jesus Christ, the Father of mercies and God of all comfort, who comforts us in all our affliction, so that we may be able to comfort those who are in any affliction, with the comfort with which we ourselves are comforted by God.

Romans 8:38-39 For I am sure that neither death nor life, nor angels nor rulers, nor things present nor things to come, nor powers, nor height nor depth, nor anything else in all creation, will be able to separate us from the love of God in Christ Jesus our Lord.

Psalms 18:6 In my distress I called upon the Lord; to my God I cried for help. From his temple he heard my voice, and my cry to him reached his ears.

Psalms 33:20-22 Our soul waits for the LORD; he is our help and our shield. For our heart is glad in him, because we trust in his holy name. Let your steadfast love, O LORD, be upon us, even as we hope in you.

Philippians 1:6 And I am sure of this, that he who began a good work in you will bring it to completion at the day of Jesus Christ.

Philippians 4:6-7 ...do not be anxious about anything, but in everything by prayer and supplication with thanksgiving let your requests be made known to God. And the peace of God, which surpasses all understanding, will guard your hearts and your minds in Christ Jesus.

*1 Peter 5:6-7 Humble yourselves, therefore, under the mighty hand of God so that at the proper time he may exalt you, casting all your anxieties on him, because he cares for you.*

## The Expert Sufferer

When your kids, especially older kids, suffer they tend to look to others who seem to struggle with the same things. They look for commiseration to show themselves they aren't alone. And so they look to the tortured lives of their friends to authenticate their own suffering. But, if they have lived in a home where suffering isn't the focus then they are less likely to call it suffering, and so less likely to turn to their tortured friends for commiseration.

You've seen it time and time again, parents who swoop in to ease the pain of their toddler. Who, when seeing a potentially painful situation immediately raise the red flag of danger and ask, "are you okay?" These three words draw attention to the suffering and ask the child to focus in on the pain rather than to brush it off and to move on. As a result, nine times out of ten, the child begins to cry and complain after the parent asks the question, not before, about the very thing the parent was quick to point out. But when a parent is less quick to draw attention to the potential for pain, the child seems less likely to experience any pain at all.

We have practiced this with our daughter from the beginning. And not only have we refused to make everything a trial, but through the use of compassionate discipleship, we have also taught to her change the subject quickly from pain to joy. When she was a toddler and something upset her or hurt her we would provide consolation as needed, but then we would quickly find something else more enjoyable that would trump her suffering. So if she cried from falling down we would pick her up, kiss her, and then show her a pretty picture, or something she had never seen before. As she got older we would do things like change the subject to something much more amazing than her temporary and minor pain or to even make her laugh. Now she has learned to change the subject in her own mind, choosing to make the good things powerful enough to override her suffering. All this is done with empathy, but also the training of her mind to help her value joy over distress and thanksgiving over complaint.

As our kids get older, this type of parenting takes on a more authoritative tone, as the stuff that distracts isn't a shiny object but the "relateability" and grace of the parent. As soon as our kids are able to experience concepts and ideas of loss and suffering, house of grace parents offer them a grace-filled understanding of their suffering. This isn't commiserating but becoming like them in understanding how that particular pain feels. For example, when your daughter cries because she misses her best friend who moved away, you could tell her to quit whining and get over it, or you could try to change the subject, but neither approach offers yourself as an expert on suffering. Because an expert would realize that this kind of pain only goes away over time. Knowing this, the most grace-filled response is one of understanding, "I know how it feels to lose someone you love. It feels awful, and it's okay to cry. But why don't we go to the park together and on the way there, we can talk about what you love about her before we jump on the swings? Getting out will be good for us." For a teenager, replace the park with her favorite restaurant and have a conversation about when your best friend moved away when you were young. See, **as an expert on suffering you know that telling someone to get over it doesn't get them over it, it just shuts them up.** But just like the stages of grief may have informed you about your own suffering, so it can inform you about theirs. In other words, allow them to suffer the same way you have, while also offering them a companion for the journey and, when they're ready, a way to move beyond the pain.

When we completely dismiss the suffering in our child's life, however small it might seem to us, we are like the debtor who was forgiven his debt but who then went and accused another of not paying the debt he was owed. We have to remember how much we have suffered and not condemn our children for walking through the same valleys we have walked through. When we're on the other side of the valley, we should be experts on sufferings of all kinds and, because of that, have empathy and compassion as we respond in grace to the condition of the human heart in our own offspring.

Your experience with suffering was meant to produce the character of Christ in you. Romans 5:3-5 says, *"Not only that, but we rejoice in our sufferings, knowing that suffering produces endurance, and endurance produces character, and character produces hope, and hope does not put us to shame, because God's love has been poured into our hearts through the Holy Spirit who has been given to us."* You can be a witness to the grace of Christ as you share in the humanity of your own children.

### An Authority on Humility

The foundation of righteousness is humility. It all starts with our humble surrender to the Father. And as we walk the walk of faith, we repeatedly have to humble ourselves to him, remembering that humility was the very nature of the incarnate Christ. This humility that Jesus then calls us to isn't reserved for adults or there would have been some caveat to the words "Do nothing from selfish ambition or conceit, but in humility count others more significant than yourselves. Let each of you look not only to his own interests, but also to the interests of others" (Philippians 2:3-4). So if this doesn't apply to our children as well, we need to adjust the text to read, "in humility count others more significant than yourselves, except children." Clearly this isn't the nature of God's Word, to demand human-inserted caveats to commands.

But how dangerous it is to a parent to behave humbly with their own child, considering them "more significant!" The first danger we assume is that we will spoil our children, worship them, adore them too much, and become the permissive parent. But the permissive parent isn't acting in humility but in selfishness, as they adore their child for how they make them feel, for the payoff they get for being lenient, for the peace, the affection, or the adoration they receive in return. But humility isn't self-seeking; it has no desire to serve self, but dies to self and fully embraces the will of God in everything. Therefore, humility does not serve to spoil the child but to teach the child the very nature of Christ.

The second obstacle to embracing humility is the fear of giving up our power. This fear feeds a lot of the things we do as parents; considering others more significant generally signifies a transfer of power. By way of example, giving up a seat to another signifies their importance over ours. You see this when a man on a crowded bus gives up his seat for an elderly woman. But his considering her more significant does nothing to decrease his power, on the contrary, it confirms it as he reveals his power of self-control, kindness, goodness, and humility. The man who fails to give up his seat, but pridefully holds onto it does more to damage his image and the respect others have for him than the one who jumps up to serve another that is weaker or smaller in stature. So why would we imagine that humility with our kids would damage our image and assault our power? The Bible makes it clear that in fact the opposite is true, "One's pride will bring him low, but he who is lowly in spirit will obtain honor" (Proverbs 29:23).

When you think of a truly humble or meek person, you tend not to think of an authoritative one. And so in relationship to our children we somehow sense that we have a free pass on the practice of humility. After all, humility only serves to reveal our weaknesses and to shine light on our failures and how can that be good for our position as parent?

Unfortunately when we reject humility as an essential part of the parent/child relationship, we embrace it's opposite; pride. And when that happens we become an unconfessed hypocrite in our children's eyes. After all, they have a front row seat to our failure. But when we refuse to act humbly and to confess our sinfulness and error we set ourselves up for disaster (see Proverbs 16:18).

The irony of it all is that when we pervert the gospel of grace with pride, we end up humiliating ourselves in the process. Jesus said, "For everyone who exalts himself will be humbled, but the one who humbles himself will be exalted" (Luke 18:14). Isn't it ironic that the very thing we seek to avoid in rejecting humility in front of our kids is the very thing that we will end up with whether we like to admit it or not?

The end goal for a humble parent is the glory of God and, practically speaking, it's to be an example and a model for how our child should grow up and treat others, in humility. We have to consistently remind ourselves that we suffer from the same sickness as our children and that no amount of training in manners, etiquette, or achievement will heal the sickness of a sinful heart like the humility of Christ. Since a parent has godlike power over a child, when that parent humbles himself to walk with their child through the aches and pains of growing up as a little sinner, the humble parent is able to show a more loving picture of the humility of Christ to their child. And when that happens, their relationship doesn't struggle under the same strain as the parent who rejects humility as "bad for business" does.

## Shame Has No Place in a House of Grace

Some years back it became in vogue for some parents to parade their children's sins before the world. Too many moms and dads attempted to bring public ridicule upon their children by labeling their sin on a sandwich board and making them wear it in public. More recently, shaming on social media has replaced the sandwich board or cardboard sign as the shaming instrument of choice.

One of the gravest mistakes that parents make is perverting humiliation by using shame as a weapon of power and as a modifier and motivator for "right" behavior. But one of the primary responsibilities of a Christian parent is to teach the gospel, that Jesus has removed our shame, nailing it to the cross. Yet even so, many of us still covet shame as a teaching tool.

We've got to understand that shame serves a very great purpose but only when it is godly shame (guilt or sorrow) as we saw earlier in 2 Corinthians 7:10, "Godly sorrow brings repentance that leads to salvation and leaves no regret, but worldly sorrow brings death" (NIV). This godly sorrow is brought on by way of internal conviction of the Holy Spirit, not through the external pressure of the world, even the external pressure of the parent. When we attempt to manufacture shame in our children, we remove the healing action of godly sorrow that leads to true repentance. Counter-intuitively, we create in our children the deadly sorrow that further alienates us from them and proves to them that the way we deal with each other is inconsistent with the Bible that we claim to adore.

When we parade around the sin of others, making a mockery either of our own children, spouse, family members, or friends we operate in the sin of pride. Not only passing judgment on their sin but also handing out conviction and punishment. We reason that parents are meant to ensure their bad behaviors are arrested and that amends are made, thus teaching them morality and faith. But teaching them to act in morality without revealing to them the depth of the Father's love for them builds a foundation of self-protection and self-interest that feeds pride and rejects the very humility that saves us. We have to remember, "God opposes the proud, but gives grace to the humble" (James 4:6).

The use of shaming or making our kids feel guilty in order to teach them is bad theology because it distorts the purpose of guilt and creates a new category, which, as I've already written, I call bad guilt. This bad guilt is any guilt that doesn't drive us into the arms of grace and leads us to true repentance. True repentance isn't made for the sake of acceptance or to reduce punishment, but for the sake of the love and remorse we feel for offending such a great God. When we put bad guilt on our children, we might start with their true guilt for sinful acts against God, but we then pervert that guilt when we tell them that guilt requires anything other than the spilled blood of Christ. If your child is taught that their guilt requires public humiliation, then the pattern of human-imposed shame for both truly sinful acts and even relational or emotional failure gets imprinted on their hearts. And from this bad theology comes all sorts of self-destructive behaviors that are meant to inflict punishment and to remove the sense of guilt that only God's grace can remove. People, who suffer from addiction, self-mutilation, and other guilt-fueled conditions of the heart, most likely learned at some point that punishment had to be inflicted in order for guilt to be forgiven. And all of this could have been avoided had the truth about guilt and grace been truly understood.

On a side note, of course this same line of reasoning does not apply to civil disobedience. The government's laws are set up for natural law purposes, to keep order and promote civilization. They are not meant to spiritually parent our children or us. And that is the distinction. The government punishes lawbreakers in order to protect the community. We disciple our kids in order to promote the gospel. And living by the gospel inevitably leads believers to respect civil laws unless they contradict the gospel.

In 1 John 1:9 it says that, "if we confess our sins he is faithful and just to forgive us our sins." This is the end to our guilt, not a piling on of shame in order to truly drive the point home or make an example of us. If God, in all his wisdom, didn't demand that guilt serve it's time, if he didn't insist that the death of His son plus repeated shaming of our sins was needed then why would we impose this false doctrine on our children?

The foundation for the authoritarian parent is pride. "Don't do as I do, do as I say." It is parenting from the center of self. And it establishes the emotional life of the family based on performance in order to get good results. So the cry of "stop that right now you're embarrassing me," is something the humble parent would never say. We lose all authority on God when we act on pride and demand more of our guilty children than God does while withholding grace. When humility isn't the filter by which we parent, our pride does more to drive our kids from true faith than any "liberal" agenda ever could. The enemy doesn't have to do any work in the life of your child as long as you are parenting in pride and demanding that your kids not only honor you, but not embarrass you or cause you any emotional grief, or physical inconvenience.

\* \* \*

As adult parents, many times we do things for people we love less than our children that we won't do for our kids because we want to train them in doing things themselves. So the kids ask for a drink and we say, "get it yourself." But when your guest asks, we jump up and get it. Imagine your funeral. Do your kids eulogize "dad taught us that perfection was the goal and that failure was not an option" or rather, "my dad was selfless, he was humble, he was a servant, he was hospitable not only to strangers but to his own children. He was never too busy, nothing was beneath him"?

If we are fearless enough to apply all of God's counsel to our relationships with our children, then we have to see that it is our lowly spirits, or humility, that leads to honor. And it's that honor that we desire from our children so that they might live a long life, so then it's most naturally achieved through our humility with regards to them. Romans 12:10 says, "Love one another with brotherly affection. Out-do one another in showing honor." Let this sink in: you and your children will be co-heirs in Heaven. They will not be under your authority; you will be a brother or sister with them. I know this is mind-blowing, but walking in humility with your child is the opposite of losing power with your children, it is growing grace-based power as you share the very gospel of grace with them in your humble responses in and to their lives.

## An Authority on Justice and Mercy

Being an authority on mercy starts with being an authority on justice, which most of us already are. Justice is almost innately woven into our souls as the exclamation "that's not fair!" pours out of our pores from the time we could first talk. But being an authority on justice has less to do with receiving it and more to do with offering it. In order to become an authority on justice in your kids' eyes, you have to be seen as just. While this might sound like a contradiction to grace, it is not. Justice does not mean that every disobedient act must be punished; justice from the child's perspective involves fairness. The parent who is an authority on justice is non-partisan, that is to say that they do not always side with one child over the other, with their spouse over their child, with self, with convenience, or with the standards enforced by others. When kids can trust in not only the justice of their parents but, more so, their mercy, then it's in that kindness that manifests itself as fairness and trust. Children find themselves in safety, as they trust their parents in return.

I often see this factor at work in the lives of parents raising multiple children. Realistically, most parents will say (to no one but themselves) that they have a favorite child. This favorite child seems to bring them the most joy and the other kids notice it. Many times this is the oldest, youngest, or the one daughter in the midst of a bunch of boys or vice versa. This partiality spells unfairness to the other children and leads them to distrust in the parent/child relationship. This is so prevalent in families that I find it very hard to name more than a handful of parents who have not fallen into this unjust trap of playing favorites.

Justice is also the ability to have a heart for the nature of your child, their temperament, and their strengths and weaknesses and to be fair in dealing with their failures. When you deal in mercy with their fears and their mistakes without making it all about you and your needs or expectations, then you don't fall into the trap of expecting their failure and planning their punishment.

By way of example, when we took our then seven-year-old to a water park one summer, she decided that she was ready to slide down the tallest slide there, as long as I went with her. So we made the long trek to the top of the slide, big plastic raft in hand. As we waited in line behind a lot of older kids the realization of the approaching entrance to the tube began to sink in. She watched the couple in front of us slide down the chute and suddenly she began to back up and whimper. She couldn't do it. While I knew that she *could* do it and might actually want to do it again and again after just one attempt, I knew that this slide wasn't what was most important, what was most important was that she could trust me, that she could feel safe with me and know that I would treat her fairly. And so we put down our raft and made our way back down against the upstream of kids clamoring up the stairs. When we got to the bottom her mom didn't look disappointed or ask, "what happened?" but she said, "I don't think I could have done it either at your age sweetie. Let's go try that one." And we all ran off for a shorter and much less scary slide. It might be helpful here to let you know that a year earlier, she wouldn't even attempt one small tube; we did the same thing with her the year before! My flesh was tempted at the time to say, "what a waste of money!" or "how embarrassing!" But because we used the money spent to disciple her and become an authority on mercy, she trusts us not just on water slides, but in the more important areas of life as well.

When your kids know they can trust you to treat them justly, to not allow your expectations for them outweigh their level of ability, and offer mercy as a compassionate authority on justice, then they will forever see you as their champion, as the one they can go to when they just can't do a thing. The lessons they learn by way of grace are more important than those they learn by way of demand or condemnation. Now, this is not to say that we cannot and do not encourage our daughter to do hard things, we do, but when those hard things are appropriate and foundational to her faith life, then we encourage her in love. But when those things are inconsequential to the life of Christ in her, then our justice serves to define the grace of God when we side with patience, mercy, and kindness rather than harsh demand and performance.

Justice is a part of the very nature of God. He is a just God and, as his children, we are meant to serve justice ourselves. Justice has to be understood not in terms of a judicial system that doles out punishment but in terms of grace. Because this side of the cross, the justice we most often think of, in terms of punishment, has already been laid on the Savior. If that weren't the case then wouldn't your sins deserve just as much punishment as your children's? But yet at the end of the day when you review your sins do you whip yourself with a cord and serve your punishment, or do you simply confess your sins and accept His grace? Justice requires punishment for sin, no question, but this justice was satisfied at the cross. So the justice that remains for you is to be fair, to refuse to listen to the flesh, that may favor one child over another, and to not put demands on your children that push them to performance over faithfulness and love.

Justice requires an examination of your priorities. What is the most important thing for your child's life? What do they need to understand above all else? Your treatment of them will reflect your answer to that question. If you answer that they know and understand the love of God, then you will act decidedly different than if you answer with understanding, growth, or mastery in any other area.

### An Authority on God

A.W. Tozer once said that the single most important thing about a person is their thoughts on God. And I couldn't agree more. Who we think God is defines our lives; how we live, love, and how we die. When we first become believers our thoughts on God are limited. We know he loves us, we know he died for us, and we know he will help us. But beyond that we are learning daily who he is as a being. And the first place that we tend to look for our definition of God is to our parents. That's a scary prospect for us humans; defining God to our offspring. What an enormous and important task, but for every person on the planet it is unavoidable. Even the delinquent dad teaches his child something about God, not the correct something but something that will shape their view of who God is for much, if not all, of their lives.

As parents we are the original authorities on God to our children. It isn't until they begin to see how much our actions disagree with the grace of God of the Bible that they start to question our love and authority. And when they question our love and authority, they begin to question our God. For any parent who wants to share the One True God with their child, there must be an equal desire to know more about this God.

Now, you might say, how can I be an authority on God? I haven't been to seminary or Bible college, I haven't even read the Bible all the way through yet! While I understand your desire for an expert to teach your child, the truth has to be said and that is that everyone is a theologian. We all have a definable theology that we may not be able to voice concisely but that we live out on a day-to-day basis. Our theology is revealed in what we worship, who we worship, and why we worship that thing or person. And we worship whatever we obsess over. It is our obsession for a thing, person, or idea that leads us to worship. And our obsessions, as parents, are teaching our kids more about our gods than any Sunday school class ever could.

If we want to become true authorities on God to our children, then we have got to know him ourselves, not know *of* him, but truly know him. We have to have a right view of who he is in all his power, wisdom, and strength, his eternal and self-existing nature. We've got to have a proper understanding of his nature so that it informs us not only of who he is but then who we are in light of that revelation. But knowing who God is isn't as easy as doing your homework because it is God himself who reveals himself to us. So I'm not talking about becoming an authority on Bible trivia but on begging God for more of Himself that you can share him with the world, especially the world inside your home.

We know who God is because of our experience with him, and our experience with him defines our approach to helping build the faith of our children. We are the first and most powerful teachers in the faith-life of our children. And the truth we must grasp is that they don't learn everything you teach them but mostly what you're excited about; this is impressed upon them deeply as they watch you day-by-day. In your life, what is being impressed on your child? Where is your passion and your obsession? And what is it teaching them about who God is?

As an authority on God, a parent serves as a sort of an ambassador to God, His representative here on earth. And because of that we represent our Father by imitating him (see Ephesians 5:1). I was once meeting with the pastor of a really large church; this was just before I married Hayley. I had flown in to meet with him for just one hour and train him in some Bible software he used and I happened to work for the company. He welcomed me into his office and told his assistant to hold all his calls. But a few minutes into our meeting, his door swings open and it's his teenage son. The pastor leaped up to greet him, introduced us, and asked him, "What's up?" His son wanted to go hiking with his friends and needed permission. The pastor, the father, said sure but to be home by a certain time and he wished he could go with him. After his son left the office, the pastor turned to me with a smile and said, "sorry about that, but not really. I have constant access to my Heavenly Father, so to the best of my ability, I want my son to have the same." I was so deeply affected, not just by the pastor, but at the notion of raising a child with a right view of God's accessibility to His children that I told Hayley the story soon after we were dating that that was the kind of father that I wanted to be.

Becoming an authority on God shows up nowhere more vividly than in the fact that God is always available to us, always. There is never something or someone else who supersedes his child, who is higher on the list. He is always there for his children whenever we call, day or night. And as people who want to teach our kids about who God is, we have to determine ourselves to become a sort of paramedic, tow truck driver, spiritual help desk, and 12-step sponsor all wrapped into one in our children's lives. This is an authority figure kids will consistently come back to, even prodigals.

## An Authority on the Gospel

As believers the gospel is important, no, paramount, to all of us. And there is not a believer who would say otherwise, but oftentimes, subconsciously we view the fruit of the gospel as more important than the gospel itself. That is to say that we spend our efforts focused on the fruit of obedience, faith, and even salvation in our lives to the exclusion of the Savior. The gospel is meant to be our focus, that is Jesus Christ crucified, resurrected, and reigning. Once we accept that, it's only natural for us to say, "Ok, so what do we have to show for this amazing truth? And how do we get more of it?" After all Jesus told us that we will be recognized as His by the fruit in our lives (see Matthew 7:20). We know this and so we feverishly do all we can to assure the salvation of our children by diligently pursuing their first confession of faith, their baptism, and their obedience as if the fruit is grown not out of the Spirit but out of our determination as parents to make them into well-behaved, good Christians. We want only the best for them and so, just as we do in our own lives, we jump to the to-do list in an effort to fast track the fruit we so desperately want to see. And then rather than wait on the Spirit to reveal truth to our children, we convince ourselves and them with our checklist. Magic prayer? Check. "Please" and "thank you?" Check. Honoring your parents? Check. We make up all kinds of substitute to-dos in order to hurry our kids salvation, to assure their final safety and their immediate obedience and maturity. But to this common and subconscious practice, God speaks these words of relief, "Are you so foolish? Having begun by the Spirit, are you now being perfected by the flesh?" (Galatians 3:3) This question should be a relief because it means that it isn't by our own power or cajoling that our children are either saved or brought to authentic obedience. But this is the true source behind all the fruit in our lives, found here in Jesus' words, "Abide in me, and I in you. As the branch cannot bear fruit by itself, unless it abides in the vine, neither can you, unless you abide in me. I am the vine; you are the branches. Whoever abides in me and I in him, he it is that bears much fruit, for apart from me you can do nothing" (John 15:4-5).

Any attempt to insist on fruit in our kids lives serves only to take away our authority on the gospel, because the gospel insists, "if righteousness were through the law, then Christ died for no purpose" (Galatians 2:21). That's why a humanistic gospel or prosperity gospel in parenting is so destructive; they both focus on growing the fruit for the fruit's own worth, rather than the fruit being a supernatural outpouring of the love and worth of something infinitely greater. When we become authorities on the gospel, we teach our children the true source of fruit, obedience, love, and faith. When we recognize that all have sinned and fallen short of the glory of God, and that includes our kids; when we admit that no laws in any house in the world could generate the genuine fruit of the gospel in our homes, then we surrender to the only One who can truly generate the life of faith and fruit in our children, and that's faith in Christ and the work of his Holy Spirit.

Good secondary things elevated to primary things are bad things. So even the desire for our kids to be obedient and godly, faithful and consistent, are corrupted when we make them the grounds for their goodness and acceptance. We cannot be good enough to be accepted by God and that's why we need Christ and the same is true for our kids. So when they fail, when they sin, when they rebel, the wise parent remembers the gospel and finds no need to react in any way that is inconsistent with that same gospel. If this isn't clear just yet, then let me just say that the definition of anything inconsistent with the gospel is called sin. When the actions of others lead us to sin, then we have rejected the gospel in favor of the law, and have taken our eyes off of the Savior.

But a more faithful reaction to the failure of others is the same reaction the Father has to our failure: grace. When we fearlessly offer grace, love, kindness, and self-control when others sin, while recognizing the sin for what it is - an assault against God and God alone - we are able to grieve with our children. But we can also rejoice in the gospel of grace that can be applied freely to their lives when they agree that they have sinned and are willing to embrace the forgiveness of the Father.

When we fail to apply the gospel to the mistakes of our kids, we are trying to make good little sinners who act how they should, all the while having hearts that are strangers to the gospel. When we aim for obedience, our methods and our hearts are dramatically different than when we aim for the amazing grace of the gospel. In this message there is freedom and relief from the continual battle of parenthood that pits child against parent, so instead we can stand side-by-side with our children in awe of the amazing grace of God. When your aim is the gospel, your priorities in life are changed and when your priorities in life are changed, you become an authority that your kids will run to when sin encroaches on their lives.

\* \* \*

### "Yes, grace but..." - Questions from a Reader

*Q: I want my kids to respect me. Doesn't confessing things like my bad choices erode that respect? And isn't it just encouraging their sin when you celebrate their confession?*

Let's take those in reverse order. Celebrating confession doesn't remove consequences. It's just the first step in the process of discipleship. First, we celebrate the transparency and take advantage of the moment, deeply ingraining the child's "want" to live in the light. Once that confession has been celebrated and some time has passed, even just an hour or two, then the discipleship continues as the topic of their sin comes up, after the emotions have died down. This allows you to disciple out of wisdom, love, and empathy instead of anger, emotion, and betrayal. Separating the celebration of confession reinforces confession, as James 5:16 puts it, as a healing process.

Being removed from the heat of the moment also allows children to participate in their own discipleship. Teaching them how to fish, i.e. how to rebound from sin when you are no longer around to catch their disobedience and to disciple them. With regards to respect, let me say that I respect people that are rooted in reality, and the reality is that we all sin. If we misrepresent ourselves to our kids, then we show ourselves as experts on projecting perfection or being respectable liars, respectable half-truth tellers. What is respectable and commendable is someone who trusts God with their self-image and walks shoulder-to-shoulder with their child. Empathy and being able to relate to what your child is going through builds respect, instead of disrespect and hypocrisy.

*Q: I work in law enforcement so, yeah, you can probably guess my problems with my kids and their issues with authority. I find it really hard to turn off "cop" me and everything that goes with it when I put my Dad hat on after I get home. So I guess my question is, "Help?"*

You're not alone. I know a number of men and women in law enforcement and the parenting challenges that pop up are intense. I'm not a cop but it's easy for me to be the enforcer of all in my kingdom. Believe it or not, I see a lot of parallels between pastor parents and cop parents; both love the law for a living! At least cops like you are tasked with enforcing the law; no such directive is given to pastors but we do it anyway. I guess my general answer to your general question is this;

spend time with your kids doing what they like to do. Do this repeatedly without bringing up anything heavy. Avoid argument at all costs. After three or four successful "dates," open up about how and why you became a cop and be honest. If it was about the power trip or that girls liked the uniform, tell them that. Next, tell them about a time you weren't sure you made the right choice becoming a cop. Maybe it has to do with when you met your spouse or when you had kids. Be vulnerable. Let them ask questions. Don't dodge them. Ask them what career they wish you had. Laugh. Tell them how much they mean to you. Confess and apologize for being harsh and wearing your uniform (figuratively) in the house. Talk about grace and how amazing it is and how you need it just like they need it but you're going to step up and lead and offer it first. Think about this next statement, pray over it, apply the gospel to it, read the next chapter and apply that too and, when you're ready, tell them there's nothing they could do that would stop you from loving them.

I hope that helped. Thank you for being a first responder in your child's life. I pray you will disarm your little purpetrators with grace.

# 6

# THE NINE MARKS OF A DISCIPLE

*When God gives any man much grace, it must be with the design that he may use it for the rest of the family." Charles Spurgeon*

IN THE TV SHOW NANNY 911, the British-born nanny goes into homes where parents are having trouble with their children and helps them to make a change. When she gets there, she spends the day watching the interactions between parents and children, and after that she knows all she needs to know about what's causing their trouble. In the same way, I could walk into a family and within a few hours tell you exactly how they are discipling or failing to disciple their kids. That might sound arrogant at first blush, but it isn't a magic formula, my years of child rearing, or my innate sense of discernment that enables me to do this, but an understanding of the nine marks of a disciple that quickly and easily reveal the depth of discipleship that is taking place and where it is lacking.

In John 15, Jesus tells us how we can identify a disciple of Christ. At the beginning of this chapter he is teaching his about abiding in him as the vine so that we can grow fruit and in verse 8 he says this, "By this my Father is glorified, that you bear much fruit and so prove to be my disciples." How do we prove to be his disciples? By bearing much fruit! Not by having some of the fruit in our lives by our natural disposition, but by bearing much fruit of the Spirit. The characteristics of this fruit is explained in Galatians 5:22-23, love, joy, peace, patience, kindness, goodness, faithfulness, gentleness and self-control. These are the evidence of the Spirit as it reveals itself in our relationship with others. Jesus reaffirms this evidence when he says, "By their fruit you will recognize them." (Matthew 7:16, NIV) Jesus reminds readers that we can easily tell the kind of tree we are looking at by the kind of fruit that grows on its branches. And the way to know if you are looking at a growing believer is by seeing all nine aspects of the fruit of the Spirit growing in their lives. So how can we judge the effectiveness of the discipleship we are giving our children? By the amount of fruit we find growing in our homes, both in our own lives and in the lives of our children.

You see, when we grow the fruit of the Spirit in our lives we offer it to our children. In other words, we act in the Spirit rather than in the flesh, and as we do we spiritually feed this same fruit. In her book, *The Fruitful Wife*, Hayley gives the visual of a fruit tree and asks readers whom this tree grows its fruit for. For itself? This sounds ridiculous; of course a fruit tree doesn't eat its own fruit. But it grows fruit for those that would come around it and eat. And the same goes for parenting since the ones we feed the most with our fruit, be it of the Spirit or of the flesh, are those that are closest to us, usually our children.

So the fruit we produce, they consume and, in turn, reproduce in their own lives. And if the fruit in our lives is joylessness, impatience, and a lack of self-control then their flesh is being fed more than their spirit. And we've all heard the expression that you are what you eat. So is it any wonder that our kids are argumentative, difficult, and disobedient when that is the same fruit that we feed them day in and day out? As we disciple our children, our goal is to help them not only digest the fruit of the Spirit but to grow it in their own lives. And since a child cannot be what they cannot see, we need to ask God for more of the fruit of His Spirit in our homes.

The idea that you can tell a tree by the fruit it grows implies that we all are growing fruit of some kind, whether it's the fruit of the Spirit or its opposite, the fruit of the flesh. So it would stand to reason that we could discern what kind of discipleship that is taking place in our homes by taking a look at the fruit we feed those around us as well as the fruit our children are growing. My wife and I did this self-check a few years ago and didn't like what we were growing. So I'm not writing on this topic as a clinical observer but as an active participant in the fruitlessness of life in the flesh. My impatience in an absence of kindness, my yelling a rejection of gentleness; I could go on and on but I won't. Suffice it to say that I realized that my fruit was rotten and I needed the Master Gardener to replant me so I could feed my daughter (and my wife) the good stuff straight from the Vine.

One of the best ways to see if you have created a House of Grace for your kids is by looking not only for the nine marks in the fruit of the Spirit but by also looking for their opposites, what we call the nine marks of the fruit of the flesh, and those are selfishness, complaint, conflict, impatience, mercilessness, immorality, unfaithfulness, pride, and self-indulgence. By looking honestly at the mood of your home, you can start to change the environment from gracelessness to grace by choosing to reject the fruit of the flesh. This needs to happen both in yourself and in the lives of your children, not through an all out food fight, but by harvesting the fruit of the Spirit in grace so they can learn from you. Of course you have to believe that children learn more from observation than from explanation in order to buy into this. Because we aren't just talking about teaching them the fruit, but giving them the fruit to taste so that they will want to attach themselves to the Vine and grow it themselves.

So where do we go then to learn to prune the fruit of our tree? How do we stop the growth of the fruit of the flesh and instead grow an abundant crop from the Spirit? Let me answer this by talking about the first aspect of the fruit that makes the list, and that is love.

## Love

When asked, the average person will say that the opposite of love is hate. And while hate is certainly an opposite to love it does not encapsulate all of the opposites of love. Recently, some have ventured to say the opposite of love was indifference. That's better. But my wife and I have long posited that the best antonym to love is selfishness. When our "love" for another is rooted in what we get out of it then we love ourselves first; we love them only in order to love ourselves.

The first business of the Christian parent is to teach our children to love. It isn't to teach them etiquette, to make them straight-A students, or the best athletes. It isn't to create future pop stars or to get them into the best college. The parent's chief end is the same as man's, to bring God glory (see 1 Corinthians 10:31; 1 Peter 4:11). And the way we do that is by loving God with all our hearts and by loving our neighbor as ourselves (see Deuteronomy 6:5). This purpose then implies that a part of that chief end is helping our kids to forsake selfishness. Selfishness draws them away from love and puts the focus on self, on the flesh.

As a fruit of the Spirit (see Galatians 5:22) love is an offspring, a by-product of the Spirit Himself. It is not a work of the flesh. Certainly the flesh can love, but the kind of love we want to reveal to our kids is the fruit of the Spirit kind of love. And this kind of love cannot be manufactured or ordered by the law. No boundaries, rules, or chore chart will ever plant this love. Since the flesh does not generate love, it cannot be awakened by the law (see Galatians 3:3). And any attempt to manufacture it in the flesh is simply a work-around that generates the appearance of fruit without actually being the fruit. This self-generated fruit stays ripe and doesn't rot only as long as we don't falter; good luck with that! In fact, as long as the love we are teaching is based on performance and law, the ultimate goal of our children will be self-protection, not love.

Please understand, I am not saying that teaching the actions of love is a waste of time, or even unbiblical. All children need to understand the fruit of the Spirit and its opposites. They need to be taught what the Spirit loves and what the Spirit gives to us. But when we fail to teach them that the source of their love isn't the law but the Spirit, we value morality over the gospel. And we end up teaching them selfishly motivated love. This love then infects all of their future relationships as it is planted in the flesh rather than in the Spirit.

In the book of 1 Corinthians, love is defined like this, "Love is patient, love is kind. It does not envy, it does not boast, it is not proud. It does not dishonor others, it is not self-seeking, it is not easily angered, it keeps no record of wrongs. Love does not delight in evil but rejoices with the truth. It always protects, always trusts, always hopes, always perseveres." (1 Corinthians 13:4-7, NIV) This passage has been the most quoted scripture in weddings throughout the ages, and the couples that listen to it often listen through the filter of self. They think how wonderful it will be to have someone who loves them no matter how ugly, sick or selfish they act. And love becomes not what we should do for others but what others should do for us. It becomes the yardstick by which we judge and condemn those near us who treat us harshly, inconsiderately, or with disregard of any kind.

But while these words can help us to gauge the love of another, these words are really intended for ourselves. Everyone who reads this passage is meant to apply it to themselves, to ingest the words and to marinate on them, to make them goal of their relationships. And nowhere is this seen more than in the dynamic of the family.

An important thing to notice about this passage is not only who it is directed to, the reader themselves, but also who it is referring to when it talks about loving. Who are we being taught to love? Easy, comfortable, peaceable, selfless people who always put us first? Of course not! We don't need to be told to be patient with or kind to these kinds of people. We don't need to be encouraged not to keep a record of wrongs for people who never wrong us or irritate us or reject us. No, this passage on love is teaching us that true love is all about selflessness, about putting others sins out of our minds and rejoicing with them, hoping for the best, and enduring difficult times. Yes, love, as defined by God, is selfless. The opposite of love isn't hate or indifference, but selfishness. This is stronger and more accurate than defining the opposite of love as indifference, because the authoritarian parent can claim constant attention, or love for their child in their constant correction. But their harshness and performance-based expectations firmly rejects the love defined in 1 Corinthians 13. When a parent considers punishment to be an act of love, they have to look at that act through the lens of the love God wants us to have for one another, yes even for our kids. Is it patient, kind, not easily angered, keeping no record of wrongs; does it honor others? How different would our discipline be if we filtered it through the lens of 1 Corinthians 13?

By way of gauging the fruitfulness of the relationship with our kids, we can first take an honest look at our love for them. If it has any odor of selfishness then we've got to be sober enough to say that we have failed to love our kids the way God wants us to love them, and so we have failed to disciple them the way we were meant to disciple them, in the love of God. But don't miss the grace here. There is, after all, no condemnation for those who are in Christ (see Romans 8:1), so in revealing this truth to our hearts, God gives us another taste of his grace as he leads us away from the sins of the flesh and towards a clearer understanding of the power of His Spirit. His Spirit allows us to love the way he loves us.

When the love we feel for our kids is born out of what they do for us, how they make us look, feel, hope, or dream, then we are living from a self-focused place not a love place. But in order to love our kids we have got to look at our motives and choose to love them with an authentic selfless kind of love that sees not how they make us feel but whose they are and what their purpose on this planet is.

This sense of selfish love pops up in all of our lives when we think about the idea of losing our kids, either to death or to distance here on earth. Parents who hear their children speak of their passion for missions understandably feel the desire to keep them safe. But God teaches us to love selflessly so that parenting doesn't become about us and our wants and fears, but stays in the realm of guardian of God's child, meant for His glory and not our own. How many times do we rob God of his glory by taking it all for ourselves in the lives of our children?

When a parent has the fruit of the Spirit love in their lives everything changes; the fear, the frustration, the bitterness, the short-temperedness, the exhaustion, and the stress all lose their power when love takes its proper form. But this fruit of the Spirit cannot and will not be ours until we learn that apart from the vine we can do nothing. Anytime we attempt to generate fruit independent of Jesus through the Holy Spirit, we end up with an unsustainable or even sour fruit of the flesh; an imitation love that is really no kind of love at all.

### Joy

Taking the temperature of your home when it comes to love is always a good idea. As we spot the fruit of the flesh in our lives we can start to find the places where grace can serve as a healing ointment in, not only our own lives but also in the lives of our children as well. So now, let's take a look at the fruit of joy and it's opposite, complaint. For the world, joy, or happiness as most call it, is something that is reliant on circumstances. When the world around us is good and comfortable we can find happiness, but when things go wrong it becomes a struggle to find any joy at all. But for the believer, joy is not born in circumstance but in the Spirit of God. That means that joy can be found no matter how bad things get. Even for people who are suffering greatly, joy is available, and readily so, when we rely on the Spirit instead of the world.

This is never so evident as in the lives of people suffering for the gospel. When their torturers threaten them, they can remain joyful as they consider the power and the call of the Spirit on their lives. And so when they struggle against the pain and agony of life, it isn't how they feel that lifts their soul but what they do. Joy is consummated in our actions, not our hearts. 1 Thessalonians 5:16-19 says this, "Rejoice always, pray without ceasing, give thanks in all circumstances; for this is the will of God in Christ Jesus for you. Do not quench the Spirit." So in order to rejoice, or to act in joy we have to pray without ceasing and give thanks in all circumstances being mindful of all that God has done, that he is in control, and that he can be trusted.

That means that in order to feed our kids the joy that is the fruit of the Spirit we have to be giving thanks always, which is the opposite of complaint, bitterness, discontentment, and resentment. The Spirit of God, when he comes into our lives, offers us a joy that is unshaken by the circumstances of life, even when those circumstances come at the hands of our interrupting, messy, or undisciplined children.

In a house of grace there is much joy, but where there is much punishment there is little joy. Where there is much law enforcement and disappointment there is little joy. Instead, we are left with the fruit of the flesh complaint. "But we can't be happy all the time!" You argue. "That's just nonsense." True we cannot be happy all the time because happiness is reliant on circumstances, but we can be joyful all of the time when joy is born from the Spirit who testifies and enlightens us to the glory of God in all things, in the bad and the good, in the failure and the misfortune. When we see His hand in all things, in at least he allowed things to happen, then we can set aside complaint and our joy can be endless.

Joy doesn't require a lack of pain, suffering, or grief in order to be experienced. After all, we read that we can "Consider it pure joy when you face trials of many kinds," in James 1:2. We can't use suffering as an excuse to reject joy. So many times in the life of a parent, feelings of hopelessness can be heavy. With difficult phases of parenting, it can be easy to see no light at the end of the tunnel. But in taking these opportunities to be hopeful, we speak silently about our thoughts on grace, because it is by God's grace that we are not hopeless, but hopeful; that we know that he has plans for us to prosper us and not to harm us, that he works all things together for the good of those who love him. So when your child rebels you don't have to turn your eyes down and give up hope but you can look forward with anticipation to what God will do through this rebellion. In this position, you can find the joy to offer grace to your child and not to withhold it as if to do so would encourage their conversion back to obedience.

But it must be said that we can't be honest in our joy when we are dishonest about our suffering. The fruit of joy feeds those around us not when life looks rosy and perfect, but when life is obviously difficult and sorrowful, yet we are rejoicing. We have to find within us the capacity for authentic joy, not joy that just ignores failure, sin, and sorrow but joy that rejoices with those who rejoice and weeps with those who weep (see Romans 12:15.) So hear me when I say that joy isn't about putting on a smile. It isn't an emotional cover-up that makes you look better than you feel and at night is washed down the sink as the make-up comes off. Joy isn't about covering up the doubt, hopelessness, and despair, but about seeing the hand of God actively at work in your mess and so acknowledges your suffering while thanking God for it.

Joy does far more to move the spirit of your child to the foot of the cross than your hopelessness ever could. In fact, any time that we express discontentment with our children, we slay the joy in our lives and theirs. But God insists that we should do everything without complaining (see Philippians 2:14). Discontentment, even with the spiritual progress of our children, though it might feel like training, is not true discipleship because it teaches our kids that contentment is based on the actions of man rather than the person and character of God.

Joy is the aspect of the fruit of the Spirit that brightens an entire home. When as parents our families sense our joy, the soil of their lives is more prepared for those same seeds of faith that bring our joy. But if we fail to rejoice in the Lord, if we are more hopeless than hopeful, then anything we tell our kids about the glory of the Lord will be received with understandably doubtful hearts. But when you feed your child the fruit of the Spirit joy, you disciple them with your very presence!

## Peace

My wife and I have ministered to teens for over ten years through our over forty books, speaking tours, and online outreach, and so we are well acquainted with how the teen years can affect a household.

Many point to the increase of hormone levels during adolescence to blame for the rise in conflict during those years. And because so many experience these hard times we have come to accept them as natural, even in our Christian homes. But according to God's Word, conflict is not a biblical norm, but a truly natural, or fleshly one. That means that there is great hope for the family caught in the middle of drama. And there is hope for those who are fast approaching that phase. Peace is a fruit that grows on the vine that we, as branches, are attached to. It is nourished by Christ, through the Holy Spirit, and so it is a part of the life of faith.

Yet for some reason parents have believed that the absence of peace is a forgone conclusion, at least in their own families. That is to say that we all tend to be more argumentative, defensive, and even aggressive within our own family unit than we are in the rest of our lives. And we believe that to be our destiny, the lot of the family. In fact, how many times do we as parents comment on the battle between siblings as natural, "Brothers and sisters fight, that's what they do," we say defensively. And the same goes for the parent-child battle. We accept it as normal rather than looking at it through the lens of God's Word, which tells us to "strive for peace with everyone, and for the holiness without which no one will see the Lord" (Hebrews 12:14). Even as you read this now, if you are like me, the word "everyone" sounds like it might not necessarily include our children. In fact, it's one of those verses that we can so easily apply to everyone but our children. But all of the commands of the Lord that are for relationships, in general, apply to all relationships, parent/child relationships included, perhaps even more! So peace is one of those things that God wants us to strive for with even our most difficult children.

But what is the cause of these fights and abundance of drama with our kids? According to James 4:1-4 it's this,

*"What causes quarrels and what causes fights among you? Is it not this, that your passions are at war within you? You desire and do not have, so you murder. You covet and cannot obtain, so you fight and quarrel. You do not have, because you do not ask. You ask and do not receive, because you ask wrongly, to spend it on your passions. You adulterous people! Do you not know that friendship with the world is enmity with God? Therefore whoever wishes to be a friend of the world makes himself an enemy of God."*

Grace looks at this verse and instead of using it to accuse others it applies it to us. So many times, when we withhold grace from our kids, verses like these are ones we apply only to them and not to ourselves. But the truth is that, as disciplers of our kids, our thoughts about them and our actions towards them serve to shape our relationship with them. And if we boldly apply the entirety of scripture to ourselves rather than to others, we will find the grace that God has given us to give them to be free from the flesh that is so desperately waging war with the Spirit.

If we can bring ourselves to embrace the grace of God for ourselves in looking at this passage, then we can begin to apply the balm of His Word to our own hearts. It is because of our relationship with the world and the lies it preaches that we find ourselves feeding the fuel of dissension at home. When we feed our passions, also known as our flesh, we starve the Spirit and we begin to lose the war within. The result is a weakened resistance to the strain that is parenting. And in this taking our eyes off of the Spirit we let His peace slip away.

But God offers peace to those who seek it, who trust that when their minds are set on the things of the Spirit, peace naturally flows out (see Romans 8:6). God is not a God of isolation. No, he is a God of restoration, which is evidence by the very giving of His son in order that restoration and peace might come to His children. This is a part of the family of faith, restoration. In fact, 2 Corinthians tells us, even us parents, to "aim for restoration, comfort one another, agree with one another, live in peace; and the God of love and peace will be with you."

When a family is built on grace, when the battle isn't against flesh and blood, but we apply the Spirit to our striving and differences, then we find peace. This fruit of the Spirit that we are meant to feed our children in order to plant the seeds of faith in them is not only healthy for our kids but for ourselves. But we cannot truly live in peace with others until we live in peace with God, accepting His grace and allowing the war between us to end as we let go of the sins of the past. We must trust that his forgiveness is a free gift for those who have accepted the blood of Christ. Peace grows out of this relationship and it nourishes the relationship between parent and child.

The notion that the teen years are going to be filled with argument is simply not true. In a house of grace, our children aren't prone to pull and to chafe against our law because grace has eclipsed the law. When confession isn't met with punishment or disappointment, but with thanksgiving and praise, then the spirit of peace will permeate our homes. And rather than becoming our child's worst nightmare we become our child's most important ally and influence.

## Patience

So we've looked at the aspects of love, joy, and peace in the fruit of the Spirit. Now let's consider the presence or the lack of patience in our lives. A lack of patience is probably one of the biggest stumbling blocks for any teacher, be it a schoolteacher, piano teacher, or life teacher (i.e. parent.) As children grow they are learning. Everyday they see, hear, or experience something they've yet to master and in those moments they need direction, guidance, and discipleship. But how easy it is for us all to grow impatient with the daunting amount of learning that is before us each day. As our kids explore the world around them they make messes, they break things, they get in the way, they are clumsy and uncouth, they are noisy, forgetful and demanding. In a word, they are inconvenient.

When our kids interrupt our lives and they take us off the course we had planned, they can mess up our dreams and our rest, and impatience can rear its ugly head as we see our lives moving in a direction we don't want them to go. The inconvenient truth about parenting is that being a parent means your life is no longer your own. That is because we have decided to accept the responsibility of another human being who will be dependent on us for eighteen years, if not more. This commitment, when taken lightly or forgotten, can lead to internal turmoil and stress as the tug for provision and the tug for self-fulfillment wage war against each other.

The other day when we were all driving to the mall, our daughter wanted to tell me all about the video game she was playing. She wanted to describe the entire scene before her. "There is this panda bear in the corner and a duck is sitting next to him. The walls are kind of pink." On and on she went, all the time my wife and I were smiling at each other hoping to get a word in with each other. At that moment, we could have told her to play by herself and to let the grown ups talk, and there are times when we say that, but this day I let her go on and on and lead the conversation. This is grace, listening to your kids' mundane topics of conversation when you'd rather have big people talk. You do this so that you reveal to them that their thoughts are important and you love them enough to listen to the things that are important to. Imagine living in a home where your mate wouldn't listen to your thoughts because they were too bored or had more important things to do; yet oftentimes this is how we treat our kids. But this is not how God treats our "mundane" prayers and conversations with him. How often do we drone on with the minutiae of our lives, even ignoring or forgetting what he has already taught us about his character, providence, and sovereignty? Yet he does not shush us, but listens intently and equally to our immature prayers as much as our supposed doctrinally sound ones. Likewise, in a house of grace children are allowed to be beginner conversationalists in need of practice and loving attention, and in this we offer them grace.

The grace that God offers us as His dependents is meant not only to free us from the guilt of having forgotten our responsibility as parents (when we give in into the fruit of the flesh impatience,) but it's also meant to be served to the source of our impatience - our kids. The grace we can give them in the face of their inconvenient presence is the fuel for our own perseverance and rest as we remember that they, like us, are little sinners slowly learning to grow in grace and the likeness of our Savior.

Grace gives patience room to stretch its legs because a spirit of grace is quick to let our kids learn through failure rather than becoming impatient. When we expect their sinful nature to lead them to lots of mistakes we are less likely to freak out when mistakes happen and, in this spirit of grace, we don't blow our tops because we saw it coming. But when we believe that our kids should be perfect, we set our ears to our flesh with its desires and ignore the Spirit. When we find ourselves exercising undo control over our kids, or at the very least their environment, we are rejecting the fruit of patience and listening to the flesh, which expresses itself in a desire for control. And from that desire comes complaint and angry outbursts when our plans (or their timely execution) are not kept.

When we fail to respond to the Spirit, we tend to respond to the flesh's desire for works in its place, and so reject grace. This isn't just a theological set of opposites but a practical one as well. And it is seen when we make our to-do list of such importance that the Spirit is rejected on the grounds that we are just too busy to take time to respond to offer grace, and if we did find the time well then they would just take advantage of it anyway and then our day would be shot. Grace can rub parents the wrong way because we see it as a free pass not to work. But that's not an accurate take on grace or on work. All our work, everything we do is meant to bring glory to God, and if in the process of working we reject God by putting our thoughts, our schedule or our desires over His then are work is not only useless but sinful. As parents we can certainly give our children a good work ethic, no question, but when we put work ethic over and above grace, the fruit that we grow is of the flesh and not of the Spirit and so it is most certainly never patience but impatience.

At those times when we are impatient with our kids, it helps to look at the law that we feel they are breaking. It is, after all, because of our sense of justice and their failure to do what we expect them to do (follow the law,) that we grow impatient with our kids in the first place. So in a home where impatience is more prevalent than patience, we can say that we are dealing with a home that doesn't embrace grace or the freedom that it offers those who live in it. As long as we react in the flesh rather than acting in the Spirit, we will be disappointed with the actions of our children because their works, like ours, will never be good enough (see Galatians 3:21.)

## Kindness

In a house of grace, kindness is essential. In fact, you cannot have grace without it because the two are synonyms. Kindness is often confused with how we feel about people. If we feel kind-hearted, like we like our kids, then we assume that we have the fruit of the Spirit kindness. But kindness, like grace, is unfair; it's not given because it's deserved but because it's undeserved. So kindness isn't the feeling we have towards our children, but the mercy we show to them. In other words, it's our refusal to punish them the way their sins deserve. It can also be thought of as our refusal to hurt them when what they do hurts us.

The desire to get even isn't unusual in the parent/child relationship. I can remember a conversation with a woman who would chastise her child for not cleaning her room by telling her that if she thought that was hard, imagine how hard it was for her to clean her sister's dirty diapers, or to clean up after the puppy when he pees all over the house. Rather than offering her grace and empathy for the difficulties she faced, she, being negatively affected by her difficulties, decided to teach her daughter how hard life is. As if showing her up on the challenge of life would inspire her or drive her to love her more for all of her hard work! When we use shame or mercilessness rather than empathy and kindness, we do not encourage our kids but, rather, discourage them. And if they do follow through with what we want them to, it isn't out of love for us or a sense of love for God but out of shame, and their fear of disappointing or being punished by us.

But in a house of grace, kindness offers empathy; a true understanding of the challenges that our little disciples face. After all, we've been there and are maybe still there! Surely we know how hard it is to overcome the flesh, to embrace growth and change. And certainly our offer of empathy and grace would do more to inspire them than our wrath or threats. In a home where behaviors are modified through works rather than through grace, the true gospel isn't taught but instead we teach them a false gospel of accomplishment and acceptance functionally taking their eyes off of their true Savior and putting them onto themselves.

Kindness refuses to use judgment as a foundation for discipleship. I shared Romans 2:1 earlier, but here it is again with verses 2-4 as well:

> "You have no excuse, O man, every one of you who judges. For in passing judgment on another you condemn yourself, because you, the judge, practice the very same things. We know that the judgment of God rightly falls on those who practice such things. Do you suppose, O man—you who judge those who practice such things and yet do them yourself—that you will escape the judgment of God? Or do you presume on the riches of his kindness and forbearance and patience, not knowing that God's kindness is meant to lead you to repentance?"

And this is the key; kindness is the Sherpa meant to guide you and your child to repentance; not justice, not judgment, and not punishment. In the life of faith, it's God's grace that leads us to see our sin and to want a change. So why wouldn't the same be true for our children? Why would we not more soundly convict their consciences of sin through God's riches of kindness and patience rather than through our accusation and a refusal to offer grace in the face of failure?

Our kindness, or grace, to our kids proves to them that their salvation and their worth isn't caught up in their performance. It teaches them the foundation of faith and that is the true calling of the discipling parent, to teach and live out the gospel to our children. We can't let the danger that we associate with kindness to scare us off from practicing it. Yes, it is dangerous. Yes, they might get away with things. But as they sense our Spirit and see His work in our lives, they will be drawn towards a true gospel, the gospel of grace.

In the life of faith, kindness doesn't punish the way our sins deserve; this is the true fruit of the Spirit (See Ephesians 2:1-4). And kindness doesn't always bring up past mistakes and sins by way of shaming to maintain power and control. As we see in 1 Corinthians 13:5, love "keeps no record of wrongs." (NIV) And because of that kindness always forgives as we saw earlier. Many parents quickly reject grace as being far too lenient yet, all the while, embracing it for their own sins. This practice even bleeds over onto the mistakes our kids make that aren't a question of morality but of etiquette, house rules, or any other parent-made law. When we fail to forgive their mistakes we make our parent-made law more important than Christ's blood-bought grace.

Etiquette, unlike the word of God, is continually changing and different across cultures. Established for the teaching of social norms and mores, it is meant to help us all fit in, to be considerate, and to behave properly. And so in the name of kindness to others it can be an important part of relating to others. But, like anything else that becomes more important than the gospel of grace, manners are often used with a destructive force against children who aren't emotionally mature enough to behave properly. Etiquette can be taught as a kindness to others until it becomes an enemy of grace when we refuse grace on the grounds that it would encourage improper etiquette. This effectively makes fitting in and appearance more important than love, grace, kindness, and patience. It's akin to not healing a man on the Sabbath; it makes the fruit of societal expectations more important than the fruit of the Spirit as it attempts to create things like the fruit of the Spirit through the teaching and enforcement of the law.

But when we freely offer kindness to the worst of sinners in our home, we do more to draw them into the conversation of the gospel than any Sunday School class ever could as we show them how grace manifests itself in the life of the sinner. And as they learn more about the Spirit and His fruit in their lives, etiquette and good behavior become more of a side effect than a prescription. Fruit of the Spirit kindness is meant to be the energy behind all of our social interactions, even our etiquette. And so it makes sense to disciple our kids in kindness and to see all the rest as an outpouring of that fruit.

## Goodness

Typically, if we want to define a word, we go to a dictionary. But with the word goodness, we can actually go to a source more authoritative than the dictionary, the Bible. In Mark 10:18, Jesus asks, "Why do you call me good? No one is good except God alone." And in 1 Chronicles 16:34, it says, "Oh give thanks to the LORD, for he is good; for his steadfast love endures forever!" So we see that God is good and since he is the only good one, we should rely on him to define goodness.

So what does God say goodness is? In Psalm 115:3 we read that "Our God is in the heavens; he does all that he pleases." So if God is good, and everything he does is good and he does what he pleases, then we can conclude that goodness can be defined as anything that is pleasing to God, including keeping His commandments, as in 1 John 5:3, "For this is the love of God, that we keep his commandments".

D.A. Carson, in his New Bible Commentary, says this about goodness, "*Real love is shown by a concern to do God's will. Indeed John can say that love for God is to obey his commands. John is not a legalist, but he recognizes that love is busy; it finds its natural expression in doing the things that please the beloved, and where will we find these things better than in his commands?*" So our obedience, then, is the fruit of the Spirit goodness that flows not from our own strength and attempt to keep the law but from the very Spirit that gives it life within us. When you love God, you supernaturally obey his word, and this is the point we want our kids to get to isn't it, where their obedience comes from their love for God rather than their fear of us? And just as our kids learned to talk by listening to us, so they will learn to identify goodness by observing our love for God and the outpouring of that into a life of our obedience. And nowhere do they notice this in action as much as in our relationship to them. If in relationship to our kids we practice goodness, that is, finding good what God himself finds good, and allowing His will to be our own, rather than becoming a surrogate god bent on reigning in sovereignty or in judgment over our kids, we will more effectively convey the message of grace at home. As we love God, we desire to obey his commands and as we obey his commands we may just find, by God's grace, that our children will flourish.

The culture of confession in a house of grace is an outpouring of goodness because confession follows those who make a practice of living in the light. When Jesus, who is the light of the world, infiltrates our lives, we covet light and reject darkness. And because of that, we freely confess anything that would tempt us to live with the lights off. Being aware of our sinfulness and confessing it to our kids seems counterintuitive, as I've already discussed, but it is part of goodness that cannot be avoided. Without it, our goodness is a charade, a shadow and not authentic to the goodness that can be our children's as well as our own.

Fear often plagues us as parents. We worry about our kids being good, faithful, healthy, and safe. Worry serves to keep us on our toes, or at least that's what we think. But fear is not a part of the life of faith but from a life of doubt. Rather, goodness disallows fear in our lives because fear really accuses God of dropping the ball, of not being enough so we have to step in. And our fear affects our kids' life and faith. If the God you worship weren't Almighty enough to protect those you love, then why would those you love trust that he is Almighty? In a home ruled by fear, our children quickly learn to dismiss God as either too distant to be trusted or too weak to be counted on. And while we might not think anything of the sort, our fear speaks volumes to their tender hearts.

But what does grace have to do with fear? How can we offer grace when we are too scared to move? The truth is that grace isn't just a part of kindness as we saw earlier, but it is also a part of God's providential care for us all. By His grace he promises to protect and uphold us and, yes, even our children. After all, "Who shall separate us from the love of Christ? Shall tribulation, or distress, or persecution, or famine, or nakedness, or danger, or sword? As it is written,

*"For your sake we are being killed all the day long; we are regarded as sheep to be slaughtered." No, in all these things we are more than conquerors through him who loved us. For I am sure that neither death nor life, nor angels nor rulers, nor things present nor things to come, nor powers, nor height nor depth, nor anything else in all creation, will be able to separate us from the love of God in Christ Jesus our Lord" (Romans 8:35–39).*

If this is true for us then it must also be true for our children, but it will not seem true to them if we don't show them that we believe it. When we worry over them, we describe our faith to them and, ultimately, the limitations of whom we worship. When we allow the Spirit to dominate our lives, fruit of the Spirit goodness satisfies us. It overflows from our lives into the lives of those around us and the environment in which we raise our kids becomes fertile ground for the gospel.

### Faithfulness

How much do your children trust you? How much do you trust your own parents? The answer to that question will help us to know of the fruit of faithfulness in your life. Faithful isn't just a description of a husband and wife, or of a constant tither, or good worker, but it so much more. Faithfulness says and does what is true. So faithfulness is trustworthiness. When we are faithful, those we walk through life with know they can trust us to do what we say. Our faithfulness as Christian parents teaches our kids the faithfulness of God. As those who disciple our children in faith, our lack of honesty in other areas of our lives can lead them to doubt our honesty in our teaching of faith. That's one reason why we decided early on to tell our daughter the truth about Santa. We had played Santa for the first three years of her life but then we started to feel convicted along the lines of faithfulness. Were we being faithful to a child when out of one side of our mouths we pretended a fantastic fat man in a red suit brought her gifts for being good while out of the other we told her of an amazing God who gives us gifts we could never deserve? After all, once she finds out that Santa was a lie what is to keep her from doubting Jesus to be just as much of one?

We might have been wrong to even play along with the fantasy of Santa, but when we finally figured out what we were doing, we quickly walked Addy through the game of pretend that was Christmas tradition among many and explained to her how we never would lie to her about a fictional character being real so that she could trust us when we said that Jesus was real. We then told her about Saint Nicholas the pastor and the real history of his legend and it was out of that same kindness for children that she should play along with other kids and adults who were playing pretend about Santa and flying reindeer, just like out of kindness we didn't look at the cup to her ear and scoff, "you know that's not a real telephone, right?!" In these sweet moments where we see our unintentional lack of faithfulness and trustworthiness, we are quick to accept the grace of God and to boldly turn the ship in the opposite direction without fear. And that is what is needed for faithfulness.

If to date we have proven to our kids that we cannot always be trusted to do what we say, to say what we mean, or in anyway to be trustworthy, then we can rely on the Spirit of God to change that in us and to help us to come clean about it to our kids. Faithfulness as it manifests itself in our lives proves that we are without unconfessed hypocrisy. We don't demand one thing of our kids while not demanding the same thing of ourselves. Instead, we reveal who we want them to become by the way we act and live in front of them.

Because of the fruit of the Spirit faithfulness, we prove ourselves to be reliable. And this does more than teach our kids about our God it teaches them about our love for them because children judge the depth of our love by the sincerity of our actions. When we are seen as faithful, we are seen as loving. Hypocrisy, exaggeration, and even drama make our kids doubt our love for them. They might not be able to express it well, but when they cannot trust our words to match our actions, how can they trust our love to be honest and reliable?

We are unfaithful when we make promises that we don't keep. That's why I have taught my daughter through my example to not make promises or ask for promises, but to let her "yes" be "yes" and her "no" be "no" and if she doesn't know for sure, than communicate that. For example, if she asks if we can go to her favorite restaurant tomorrow, I tell her that we should be able to do that and I'm looking forward to it. I don't promise because I know things come up; a pipe freezes or we get sick. What this allows us as parents to do is elevate the amazingness of God's promises in scripture and His faithfulness; he never changes His mind or leaves us hanging. And since I am called to be faithful, I don't make promises that I may not be able to keep. But there is one promise I have made her. When she was just a toddler and through her preschool years, I made a habit of asking her, "do you know why I love you?" She would posit an answer like, "Because I'm pretty!" or smart, or funny, or nice. To which I would say, "yes, you are..." this or that, "but that's not why I love you. I love you because you are my daughter." This is why God loves us; it's in spite of our unfaithfulness. So, to be faithful to God's call on my life as a father, I must communicate to my daughter that I will be faithful to her even if she is unfaithful. We must aspire to the faithfulness of the Father of the prodigal, faithfully waiting for, not an obedient son, but a wayward one, leaping to greet him and throw a party for his confession and return. When we fail to follow through on the things

God tells us to do and how he tells us to live, we become the prodigal in need of restoration. When we embrace the prodigal Father for ourselves but hold our kids to a higher expectation and standard, we live out of our flesh of the elder brother rather than the Spirit. It is the flesh that is unfaithful; it's prone to overcommit, to forget, and to change our minds. But when we live from the Spirit, we remain faithful to live moment-by-moment for God's purpose and we take our children on that journey. That means faithfulness includes spontaneity to be used by God when he pleases, which removes our promises from the equation when we live by the Spirit.

Faithfulness is seen not only in our actions but also in our words. When we complain, criticize, or in any way express discontentment or joylessness, we are being unfaithful. That is because we are making an accusation against God through whom all the things we are complaining about have come (see Lamentations 3:37-38). But faithfulness speaks words of encouragement, hope, thanks, appreciation, and praise. Faithfulness is not only being honest about ourselves but devoted to our God and speaking honestly about him. This is just more support for the offering of grace in our children's lives. When we speak in grace to them, we are faithful to the grace he has offered us and to His word. Our faithfulness then points a glorifying finger at a perfect God rather than detracting attention from His glory onto our unfaithfulness.

If our home is built on faithfulness of speech and action, then our kids are getting an authentic example of the life of faith powered by the Holy Spirit from one broken sinner to another. But if we prefer to sweep our sins under the rug and sugar-coat life, we will be selling our kids a load of goods that will lead them to disillusionment rather than enlightenment. And conversely, if we make much of complaint and criticism, basically accusing God of not being faithful, then we will drive our kids away from the One who would save them.

### Gentleness

In relationship to your children, would you be considered harsh? Or is there an easiness in your spirit that expresses itself in gentleness? For most of us the answer to that is "no," at least not most of the time. That's because in relationship to our kids the flesh is ever being tested, pushed, pulled and poked. When it comes to our interactions with our children and our ideas of how they should behave, what they should say and how they should speak, gentleness usually does not come naturally. And because of that it is in relationship to our kids that we have one of the greatest opportunities to practice rejecting our flesh in favor of the Spirit.

Gentleness comes from the Greek word *prautes*, which can also be translated as meekness. Neither of which are words often used when speaking to parents about their relationship with their children. But gentleness is a fruit of the Spirit that, far from being off limits to our children, is meant to feed them daily. Meekness is not a comfortable term to the modern ear, let alone to the modern parent. However, to the original readers or hearers of God's Word the Greek word *prautes* would be understood not as a negative, as in doormat or wimp, but as "strength and courage under control, coupled with kindness."[xi]

In a house of grace, gentleness is a mark of that grace because gentleness imitates Christ. He who called himself gentle, who said of himself, "Take my yoke upon you, and learn from me, for I am gentle and lowly in heart, and you will find rest for your souls" (Matthew 11:29) is meant to be our example. The thing that Jesus repeatedly expressed was his meekness before God, his complete rejection of self in elevation of the Father.

But biblical meekness doesn't come naturally. In fact the opposite is most often true as we tend to consider ourselves first and others second. At the moment that we consider ourselves first over

God and His will, over Jesus and his meekness, we begin to rebel. And when we rebel we turn to harshness, unreasonableness, rudeness, and criticism in an attempt to protect ourselves and to get what we want out of a situation. But this is the opposite of gentleness, which is first of all meek towards God, allowing him to choose what is best for us. It is our deep desire to be the master of our own domain, especially in our homes, where we often find ourselves reacting in a spirit of disdain, judgment, and faultfinding. In these moments we disregard our children as we consider our feelings more important. I'm not saying that gentleness excludes correction. I'm just saying that it includes kindness and grace in the delivery of that correction. This is laid out clearly in Galatians 6:1, where it tells us "if anyone (including your child) is caught in any transgression, you who are spiritual should restore him in a spirit of gentleness." (Emphasis added) Correction is a part of parenting but it must be done in a spirit of meekness.

When we fail to disciple our children with gentleness, we teach them that the fruit of the Spirit isn't meant for failure but success. In other words, we mistakenly teach them that we respond to the Spirit only when they are being good, but not when they have messed up. In those instances we choose to rely on the flesh. But in those moments when we serve our flesh over the Spirit, we create problems between our kids and ourselves; problems that quickly spiral out of control and turn into shouting matches, slammed doors, and hurt feelings. This battle between parent and child isn't a new one but one that the Bible addresses in Ephesians 6:4. In it we read, "Fathers, do not provoke your children to anger, but bring them up in the discipline and instruction of the Lord." The word provoke might also be translated to frustrate or irritate. And the single most frustrating thing that a parent can do to a child is to apply the law without applying the grace of the gospel. Just like a life of supposed grace given by a permissive parent without the child knowing anything about the law is destructive, so is the laying of the law without the offering of grace. And even though we've already covered this ground, it's worth noting again that "bring them up in the discipline and instruction of the Lord" must be centered on and applied through the lens of the gospel. And that means that discipline is through the training of how Christ loved us plus our context of the instruction from one big sinner loving a little sinner regardless of their performance.

In Proverbs 15:1 we read, "a soft answer turns away wrath, but a harsh word stirs up anger." Yet how many times do we exclude our kids from this wisdom, insisting that harshness is acceptable in parenting? Are we surprised then when our kids are continually at odds with us and our nerves are worn thin? Gentleness extended to our kids will mark a house of grace because grace is by nature gentle. This is because we rely on the Holy Spirit for both the grace to love our kids and the gentleness to reveal that love to them. Gentleness isn't easily offended, doesn't take things personally, and is willing to be interrupted and inconvenienced.

How many times do we as parents reject gentleness when our children inconvenience us? We do so many things in the name of convenience, including discipline. "Sit in your seat until you are done eating," we say to the two year-old who screams all through dinner. But grace looks at each child as an individual and raises them the way they were meant to go. So grace might let the young child get down and walk around while they eat, come by the table and grab something, play, then come back to eat. Grace isn't afraid. It isn't afraid that if it doesn't force adult behavior now those behaviors will never come. It trusts that God predetermined the child's level of development and he has a plan for each phase. He didn't make us all come out competent and complete for a reason. Just as you wouldn't expect a brand new believer to give a perfect sermon and do all the right things, you can't expect a baby to do everything they ought to do as an adult. When you expect your kids to behave above their age level, then you are setting them up for failure instead of success. How many things do we do in the name of convenience? Rush our kids; say "no" to their requests to stop and play with frogs, or to look at something at the store? When our answer to their requests finds its motivation in convenience it is neither love nor grace.

If you aren't sure if your home is a house of grace, one good way to start to find out is to think about ways your kids might describe you as a parent. If they would call you strict, then gentleness might not be a fruit that you offer them. When we are harsh with our kids, we offer a response that is the opposite of gentleness and, therefore, the opposite of the fruit of the Spirit, the fruit of the flesh. Gentleness in times of testing is hard to conjure up in our flesh because our flesh wants justice and retaliation. Our flesh seeks always to protect itself and to defend itself, but the Spirit isn't occupied with the flesh but the things of God. And so when we set our minds on the Spirit and allow him to affect our responses to testing, we will feed our children on the goodness of God rather than the disappointment of our flesh.

One note about "tough love": tough love is needed for extreme situations, like a child that is endangering the rest of the family. But tough love can and must be gentle and never harsh. It must be rooted in scripture but loving in hope and restoration. There are so many parenting scenarios that can't be delved into here, but remember the story of the prodigal: the father in that story let his young adult son go without bitterness or imprisonment and entrusted him to God's providence. And as I observed earlier, the son's repentant return was greeted with joy, not repayment, punishment, or penance. Such is the Father's love for us!

But how do we manage to offer gentleness when our emotions run so strong? The answer to this is the same as it would be for all of the fruit of the Spirit. We have to understand that the fruit of the

Spirit doesn't come natural to any of us, but has to be sown into our lives by the life of Christ in us. That means that when we want to offer grace to our kids, to live in gentleness with them, we have to daily go after God with all of our heart and ask him to fill us with the fruit of his Spirit so we can fill our children with the same. In addition to that we have to begin and continue the conversation with our children about the fruit of the Spirit in their lives.

Most of us fail to offer the fruit of the Spirit gentleness in abundance to our kids, but God's grace is big enough to cover this failure too. What we have to do from this point forward is rely on God every morning to teach us how His Spirit would have us interact with our children and then to share that with them, confessing our failures of the past and committing to a more gentle future.

## Self-Control

Hopefully, I've begun to convince you that the fruit of the Spirit marks a disciple of Christ and a house of grace. As the fruit comes from the life of the Spirit inside us, it feeds our kids some of that same Spirit. But if you are like me, after having seen the benefit of this fruit, you're saying, "easier said than done!" Because when it comes down to it, everyone can recognize their total lack of self-control, especially in the area of discipling our kids by how we live. In fact, if we are being honest, we can see a lack of self-control in every fruit of the Spirit. So what's the answer? Is it more self-control so that there can be more fruit? That can't be it or from that we could infer that they aren't fruit of the Spirit at all but of our own making, sweat, and toil. Since we know that isn't true we have to look at self-control differently. Self-control isn't putting your "self" in control of anything but it's controlling your "self" by means of giving self over to the Spirit to do with it what he will. That means that self-control is the ultimate act of surrendering your will, heart, mind, and self-life to the Holy Spirit.

Another way to think of it is to think of self-control as self-restraint, the holding back of your self-life, not serving it.

In Mark 8:34, Jesus says, "If anyone would come after me, let him deny himself and take up his cross and follow me." Denying self is an essential part of following Christ. And because it is a part of following Christ, for the Christian, it's a part of parenting and for the child it's a part of growing. A lot of times this self-denial comes naturally. For example, when you see a mother who will give the best of her food to her child instead of keeping it for herself. Or in the life of a father who will work long and hard in order to keep food on the table. Self-denial is generated by love.

But what happens when your feelings aren't that loving? When frustration, anger, bitterness, and the like are louder than love, self-denial is the furthest from your mind. In those moments when you "lose it," you can see just how much self-control you don't have, and how much you'd rather fight for yourself than die to yourself. In those out-of-control moments, the fruit of the flesh selfishness, joylessness, conflict, and all the rest bubble to the surface and we feed it to everyone within earshot, or sneer-shot.

While love is the foundation of all the fruit of the Spirit in the house of grace, self-control is the restraint to let God build the house through His Spirit and according to His purpose. Romans 8:5 tells us, "those who live according to the flesh set their minds on the things of the flesh." And that's the source of all of our lack of self-control; our minds become set on the things of the flesh. At home, the things of the flesh can be stuff like order, control, tradition, comfort, pride, busyness, schedules, arguments, appearances, our things, our hopes, and our dreams. When our thoughts are focused on our purposes and our will rather than the Father's, we choose self-indulgence over self-control. And when grace is withheld, power, justice, and obedience come at the cost of surrender to the Spirit. And when that happens, we embrace the law and we shut out grace.

But self-control freely offers grace because it doesn't respond to the flesh that screams for selfishness, bitterness, resentment, revenge, angry outbursts, and other emotional reactions. But when we rely on the Spirit instead of the flesh, we come under the control of the Spirit and that's when we overflow with the grace of God to our children. The truth is that most of us lack self-control because we think the fruit of the Spirit is a luxury, for those special gifted types, instead of a necessity for all of us. The fruit of the Spirit is singular, not plural. That is because they refer to one fruit, and each is simply a characteristic of that fruit, the fruit of the Spirit. It's like this, if I asked you to tell me about an orange you could say that an orange is orange in color, sweet, juicy, it smells fresh and clean, it's fibrous, and the list could go on. Each one of these descriptors isn't a fruit, but an aspect of the fruit. It's the same way with the Spirit. When the Spirit lives in you he grows fruit, and that fruit is described with those nine descriptors. So when you have the fruit of the Spirit you don't have a select few, but all of them. Now your fruit might be less juicy than others, or not as sweet, but there is no aspect of the fruit that is unavailable to you. All of it is meant to grow and ripen in the life of faith.

Don't panic if you look at your life and see that you haven't shown much fruit of the Spirit in relationship to your kids. This realization only proves that the Spirit is something you need more of and knowing that is the first step to true self-control. In order to have self-control with regards to discipling your kids, you have to start with turning your will over to God. His will and happiness have to become more important to you than your own. When that happens, self-control grows. And when self-control grows, the other fruit has more space to grow.

Of course, in the life of a child (or any human,) self-control is a long journey. But that doesn't mean that it isn't a journey they should be on. As they watch our self-control, they learn more than we could ever speak, but we still have to speak to them in moments when they lack self-control, when they indulge themselves and put self over and above others. We have to help our kids, in grace and empathy, to learn to die to self and to live for God.

Beyond observing our own self-control, we must have constant conversations on the topic. Not as a form of chastisement, but as discipleship, helping your child wrap their heart around this counter-cultural approach to life. We also have to remember that teaching the fruit of the Spirit wrapped in punishment gives the fruit a bad taste. But offering them thoughts on self-control by way of example or confession as they see instances when you fail at self-control gives the fruit a fresh and appealing taste. Then they see a real-life example of the value of self-control and the selfishness of failing to rely on it.

Self-control isn't an option for the believer. In fact, we can't look at any of the nine aspects of fruit of the Spirit and say they aren't for us. Anyone who has the Spirit living in them will have his fruit growing in their lives or Jesus wouldn't tell us that you identify a believer by their fruit. The fruit of the Spirit self-control grows in the life of faith. That doesn't mean it is perfected but it is always increasing as we learn from day-to-day to give ourselves more fully to the Spirit and to refuse our own flesh. Self-control is the aspect of the fruit that encourages all the other fruit to grow more abundantly, and it is fertilized and nourished by our surrender rather than our need for control.

## Changing your Family Tree

There is a tree in a backyard that has taken a turn for the worse. This tree has grown up crooked, tipped over to one side as if blown repeatedly by the wind or neglected by the sun that hides behind a bigger, more impressive tree next to it. So instead of growing straight and powerful, this little tree has managed to hunch over like an old man would way before its time. This tree can't support a tire swing; it can't bear what the other trees can bear. It looks awkward and ugly and threatens to crash down onto the fence that stands underneath it if something isn't done soon. But it's not the end for this messed up tree, it can be saved and helped to grow into a healthier and more upright position through some time and attention. A lot of trees have been redirected, pruned, pulled, held up and taught to grow straighter and more full simply by giving some attention to the places where the tree is lacking strength and support and by applying reinforcement.

But redirecting something as strong and deeply rooted as a tree takes time. It isn't done in a day, but it can, with patience, be straightened up and helped to become the tree it was meant to be. It's no coincidence that people often refer to their family history as a tree. Understanding that the roots of sin, and even sacrifice, grow deep into the ground and are resistant to change makes the tree a perfect analogy for our emotional, physical, and even spiritual DNA. How many times have you seen the sins of the father visited on the children for generations? It's both a curse and a natural result of one sinner raising another. And so the family tree analogy makes a lot of sense as we look at the natural tendencies in our lives as well as the lives of our offspring.

In our home, we have made the reshaping of our family tree part of our daily mission. Keeping things the way they are just because we feel powerless to change such a behemoth as our family tree is not an option for us. Since God made such a change in our lives, we are convinced that this change can and will impact the direction that our family has taken for centuries. The life of faith is, after all, a life of perpetual change towards a closer image of Jesus Christ himself. And until we see that in our heavenly lives, we have to continually work towards movement in that direction, for ourselves as well as our children.

As you read about the fruit of the Spirit, it is important that you understand the fruit more and more so that you can teach them to your children. It is after all, a great unkindness not to encourage the same fruit in our children's lives, as we want in ours. When we as parents allow our kids to feed on or to grow an abundance of the fruit of the flesh, we are discipling them in the ways of the world. And from that comes all kinds of sibling rivalries, arguments, disobedience, angry outbursts, bitterness, and the list goes on. If we look at any of the problems that we have with the behavior of our kids, we will see at the root a lack of the fruit of the Spirit. But even if they are not yet believers, they are not exempt from the need to gain knowledge about the fruit. Charles Spurgeon agreed with this declaration when he said that, "no sinner around you will be saved except by the knowledge of the great truths contained in the Word of God. No man will ever be brought to repentance, to faith, and to life in Christ, apart from the constant application of the truth through the Spirit." And as the discipler of your child, this describes your most important job, to constantly apply truth through the Spirit to your children.

In our house of grace, the fruit of the Spirit is an everyday topic. We talk about one of them, or all of them, almost everyday. That's because they're essential to the life of faith; they are the nine marks of a disciple. And as our daughter grows, she is continually finding out new ways to understand her flesh. So virtually all of our conversations with her about her troubles, her fears, her sins, and her relationships all center around her understanding of the power and the purpose of the Spirit in her life and the fruit that comes from that. If our prayer is for our children to abide in Christ, when it comes to diagnosing the daily events in our children's lives, why wouldn't the fruit of that abiding be the daily, number-one topic of conversation?

Being aware of the growth of our family tree involves opening our eyes to the sin in our children's lives as well as our own. In fact, we also have to be sober about the sins of our parents, not so we can sit in judgment of them but so that we can be equipped to better identify their spiritual DNA as it manifests itself in our lives. This involves becoming keenly aware of those things that we have always considered "just a part of who we are," our personality, our bloodline, and then being honest about how they may be the fruit of our flesh in our lives. If we continue to let personality be an excuse for the fruit of the flesh, then we will forever subvert the fruit of the Spirit in favor of self.

In a house of grace, the family tree is forever being pruned and redirected. That's because God is continually changing his children. 2 Corinthians 3:18 talks about this change when it says, "and we all, with unveiled face, beholding the glory of the Lord, are being transformed into the same image from one degree of glory to another. For this comes from the Lord who is the Spirit." If we are not changing more and more into the image of Christ then we are not attached to the vine and not living in a house of grace. Let this be the greatest yardstick to our faith; our vital attachment to the One in whose image we were made.

\* \* \*

## "Yes, grace but..." - Questions from a Reader

Q: I feel I have some of the fruit in my life, but I struggle with patience and gentleness; I can be quite harsh as a dad (and husband.) How do I grow in those specific areas?

This might be hard to read but maybe it will be easier when I confess that I also gravitate towards impatience and harshness: the absence of some of the aspects of the fruit of the Spirit in your life means there's an absence of **all** of them. That's because the nine aspects or marks of the fruit can't be separated. The Spirit doesn't give you seven and forget two. More likely, like it was in my life, the other seven are present in your life because you are producing them in the power of your own flesh. This happens when you are loving or good for what it does for you (and your flesh.) This was the number one hit-me-with-a-truck paradigm shift in my life; I was disconnected with the One that produces the fruit. In John 15, Jesus says that apart from the vine we can do nothing (including bearing fruit.) So, growing all nine marks of a disciple involves spending more time, moment by moment, attached to the vine. Spending time with Jesus and his Word, especially meditating on kindness (a synonym for grace,) will transform your heart, soul, and mind. Something as simple as applying a mental filter of "Is this fruit of the Spirit kindness?" when you interact with your kids and spouse will humble you when you discover how much a harshie like you and me operate on a frequency of unkindness. I am praying for you my friend. Will you pray for me that God will continue to kill my harsh nature?

"How you love and disciple your kids helps establish the foundation for the character of God to that child. Are you showing them a kind and gracious God who is patient beyond measure and merciful beyond belief? Have you shown them the grace of God to the level that he has shown it to you?"

— House of Grace

# 7

# BUILDING A FAITH WORTH OWNING

*"A lack of deep belief in the gospel is the main cause of spiritual deadness, fear, and pride in Christians, because our hearts continue to act on the basis "I obey, therefore, I am accepted." Tim Keller*

ANY CHRISTIAN PARENT THAT WANTS THE BEST FOR THEIR CHILD WANTS THEM TO HAVE A SAVING FAITH IN JESUS CHRIST. But this isn't a simple inheritance made possible by family bloodline, but something that is a work of the Spirit just like it was in our own lives. This turning of your spiritual life over to the Holy Spirit can be frightening because in the act of turning over control you, well, lose control. And the effort you desperately want to put into proving the value of faith to your child is ultimately powerless compared to the power of the One who saves them.

This means that we can't just teach Bible stories to our kids, and convince them to say the sinner's prayer and then think it's all good. This misguided idea of faith only leads to trouble as your child tries to get a handle on a faith that was never truly made their own. But all of this powerlessness isn't the end of the story, but should be hope for a better future. That's because once we realize that their salvation isn't our job, but the Father's, we can start to rest in His grace not only for ourselves but for our children, and in that to know that His will be done and our job is just to till the soil and prepare their hearts to receive His Spirit (see John 6:44.)

In this tilling, we've got to realize that there are phases to the spiritual lives of our children that on the surface might be despairing but once fully examined can be seen as just a part of the process. In our book, *Own It: Leaving behind a borrowed faith*, my wife and I talk about the faith of young people who grow up in Christian homes. In a home where Christianity is espoused, children learn the vernacular of faith from an early age. They often know all the answers to spiritual questions and can regurgitate biblical truth on cue; they aren't however always acting on faith but on an imitation of faith. This thing that mimics faith is a part of the healthy walk of many children until it fails to move from a faith that is borrowed to a faith that is owned. That is to say that we often start out our faith walk out of devotion and blind allegiance to those who came before us. Just like you might hear a five-year-old adamantly supporting a presidential candidate based not on their own understanding of the candidate's political platform but on their parent's endorsement, so too you also see children claiming a faith that they took for the same reasons.

Before you reject this idea as too depressing, consider the fact that this process isn't necessarily bad. How else do our children learn about their God unless they are taught? As we read in Romans 10:10, "How will they know if they have not heard?" So I'm not discounting our impressing the things of God into the lives of our children, after all as I've already pointed out, Deuteronomy 6 insists that faith be the topic of conversation on a daily, and moment by moment basis in a house of grace. We can't however look at this conversation as proof of our child's faith, nor see their acceptance of the things we teach them as evidence of their salvation, but simply as the initial road of faith that we all walk.

Knowing this can help us to parent our kids more graciously to the foot of the cross by alerting us to the fact that it's not true faith we instill in our children when we demand their obedience to God's law and they merely submit. Because as long as they are getting their power to be "good" from their desire to please us or to keep from being punished they will ultimately fail, because they do not have the power to be perfect, and when this comes to the surface, when their flesh fails them, and it will, they will begin to doubt the faith they worked so hard for.

In order to help our children stop borrowing or faking their faith to gain our approval, we have to allow them to fail. We have to show them the grace of God in the same way he has shown it to us. Without this grace in their lives, they will forever be renters of their faith, making monthly payments by way of works, rather than owning their faith through the redemptive work of the cross.

It's helpful to remember that your child is not in peril of hell because she fails to own her faith today. Fearing that only proves you don't fully accept the sovereignty of God or trust that salvation is truly an act of grace, not by works, so that we cannot boast (see Ephesians 2:8.) No, even if your child should question the things of God and say they aren't sure they believe, don't panic. Panic never saved anybody and it won't help your child. But a confident belief in the God who owns you will do more to fertilize their heart to His truths than your fear, your panic, or your demands.

When our daughter was about four-years-old, she told Hayley that she wasn't sure she could believe in a God who was self-existent. I know, doesn't sound like the vernacular of a four-year-old, but we are a Deuteronomy 6 household, so she hears these kinds of concepts about God all the time. But this particular time she was struggling with the idea that no one made God and it caused her to doubt the faith she claimed just the year before. Hayley's first instinct was panic. But she remembered what she knew about faith and took a deep breath. And her response went something like this, "I know that's hard to believe, and I can't and won't make you believe it honey. But what I can do is tell you that I am certain beyond a shadow of a doubt that he is God and that he can be trusted. Even when I don't understand what he says, I still trust him." My wife went on to testify to many of the things she had seen God do in her life, and by the end our daughter wasn't convinced but she was comforted and not guilted by her inability to understand the depths of God's being but glad to know she didn't have to. Plus, she learned a valuable lesson that she could easily delay and extend bedtime if she had spiritual questions for us! She still does this to this day and we welcome it; it is a sweet time of exploring our faith even if it delays our time together as a married couple. Discipling her is worth it.

We do more to prove the existence of God by our grace than by our law. We cannot order our kids to faith. We can order them to church, order them to read, even order them to pray, but none of this has the power to give them a saving faith, only the Spirit of God can do that. But we can help them to have a truer understanding of who God is by being determined to give up faking or borrowing our own faith. That is to say that until you have given yourself over fully to God to own your life, you haven't fully owned your faith. But when you do give up your will for His, your children will notice. Kids see who God is by how you interpret him through your words and actions and, through that, they will get either an accurate or distorted view of who God is.

If your child is struggling with their identity, if they suffer from self-hate, depression, or anger, then this altering of your thinking and their experience of your faith can greatly benefit them. That's because when your kids learn to fake their faith they never truly find the acceptance from you that they so desperately crave because, as we said in our book *Own It*, "When you are faking something for the approval of others, even the approval you get is painful because it's based on a lie, and the real you never truly finds acceptance."[xii] Faking our faith is damaging to more than our eternal security, it can damage our very psyche. When parents struggle to understand why their kids have such harsh images of themselves, when they look for answers to the darkness that plagues them, parents then have to begin to consider that darkness exists in the absence of light. It was Jesus who said, "I am the light of the world. Whoever follows me will not walk in darkness, but will have the light of life." (John 8:12) And we walk in the light when we own our faith, not when we act like we have faith in order to be accepted.

It's normal and okay, and a part of discipleship, them following Christ because you're following Christ, until the point where they don't use you as an intermediary any longer. And this point has to come. When that moment comes isn't up to us, but if it hasn't come by the time they leave your home, your job isn't done just as the prodigal's father's job wasn't done. You must pray and prepare for the day your son turns from darkness and comes home into the light. You must pray that God brings someone into their life that can build upon the foundation you laid and even repair and rebuild the faults in that foundation. God is able.

A borrowed faith is a deadly faith. "When your faith truly belongs to someone else, when you took it out of obligation or even devotion to your loved one, it makes the person you got it from the god of your life,"ˣⁱⁱⁱ When a child borrows their faith in this way, when their devotion is more grounded in pleasing you than in loving God, what you say and do can have a dramatic impact on your child. And so your failure (and we all have failures) will wound them deeply because, as the god of their life, you define not only their faith, but also who they are. And when you fail to be perfect as God is perfect their world is shaken and often times they do not recover. In these instances, the parent/child relationship can suffer, the child's relationship to others can suffer, marriages suffer, and families suffer, all because we set ourselves up as gods in our children's lives.

You see this a lot in the lives of adult children. How many times is there strain in their parental relationships? How many times do these relationships cause strife in the family unit and suffering for everyone involved? When we encourage our kids to borrow their faith by setting ourselves up as the ultimate authority in their lives, demanding their faithfulness, obedience, and allegiance we attempt to replace God in their lives and the consequence is disaster. We must beware of insisting on blind allegiance from our kids. After all, their allegiance is meant to be for their heavenly Father, "Whoever loves father or mother more than me is not worthy of me, and whoever loves son or daughter more than me is not worthy of me." (Matthew 10:37)

When your child owns their faith, it starts with their confession of faith and not your confession of faith. You cannot make that confession for them, and you can't force them to make it for themselves. But you may influence the process by being an example of true faith in their lives. And that means that the very faith that was given to you by God through His grace must do it's work in their lives through the grace you offer them as they present themselves as sinners in need of salvation.

## God First, God Second, God Third

While my parents were both alive they shared a love affair that others only dreamt of. They were devoted to one another above everyone else, even their own children. And as a result of seeing their romance, I wanted nothing else but to duplicate that same soul devotion in my own life. And so my goal for as long as I can remember was to get married and to have a person who always put me first and who I could always put first. This led me into one relationship after another where I imagined that each woman would be the one and I would give them my all, only to discover they weren't the one and so I'd move on to another. And through it all I got really good at practicing divorce as I searched for the "perfect" love my parents experienced.

It wasn't until after a failed marriage of less than three years in my twenties and a failed life into my thirties that I finally stopped searching for another person to complete me and started looking to God to be everything I thought I needed in another. As I turned my life over to Christ I started to see my parent's love affair differently. I started to see its destructive force as it taught me that I would never be first on anyone's list unless I had a wife. It taught me that love wasn't so much about serving others but serving yourself through your romantic relationship. And it gave me a warped sense of the love of God. I love my parents; I lost my dad a over a decade ago and my mom this past year. But out of six kids, all have divorced except for one who has never married. I am the youngest of six in my forties and I have the only child born into the family. Worshiping your spouse isn't healthy for you or your kids.

This problem isn't unique to a child of World War II era romantics; it's a symptom of many Christian evangelical homes where parents are taught to place a higher value and devotion on their marriage partner than on their kids. In the way of thinking where we put God first, spouse second, and kids third, we unwittingly create a yearning in the lives of our children for a relationship that will give us what we only see at home but do not experience, being first to another person.

As my wife and I minister to young people, we see this way of thought permeating many of their relationships, from the infatuation with finding a BFF (best friend for life), to the all-consuming search for their soul mate, Christian children are being taught that they will never be higher on the lovable list at home than third. And that only feeds their desires for romantic relationships in high school and beyond.

How this idea of God first, spouse second, and children third came into vogue I do not know. But many would support this saying using scriptures that point to the husband and wife becoming one flesh (see Genesis 2:24) and the husband loving his wife as he loves his own body (see Ephesians 5:28). And while I do not disagree with scripture being taken literally in these instances, I also recognize that biblical love isn't something we are meant to prioritize among members of the body. In fact, love is meant to be given without reserve to everyone, even to our enemies as we see in Matthew 5:44, "But I say to you, love your enemies and pray for those who persecute you" (Matthew 5:44). Romantic love is not given a higher priority than brotherly love according to Jesus, but love is meant to be born out of one place and one place only, our love for the Father. That is why he summed up the commandments with these words, "And you shall love the Lord your God with all your heart and with all your soul and with all your mind and with all your strength.'" (Mark 12:30)

The word "all" used in this passage describes a heart that loves God with 100% of itself. It would stand to reason then, that there is either no love left over for the rest of the world, which is inconsistent with God's Word, or it must be that loving God with 100% of our hearts is accomplished when we love others as ourselves. This is the idea that is confirmed in the second commandment that Jesus gives us when he says, "The second is this: 'You shall love your neighbor as yourself.' There is no other commandment greater than these" (Mark 12:31.) Notice that Jesus says nothing of the priority of spousal love here, but instead he groups everyone around us into this category, not making it God first and your neighbor second, as one might deduce, but loving God with *all* your heart would be God first, God second, God third.

It is out of this complete devotion of the believer's heart to God the Father that we are able to love others selflessly at all. The truth according to 1 John 4:19 is that "We love because he first loved us." Meaning that we can truly love only once we accept the love of Christ in our lives. We can love only when we accept that love and from that acceptance we in turn are able to love God with 100% of our hearts. And then because of that we can love our neighbor, or our spouse, or our children, as much as we love ourselves.

Jesus uses the idea of loving others as much as we love ourselves because he knows the depths of our natural love for ourselves and the fleshly tendency to the opposite of love; selfishness. If we are honest with ourselves and we let the Holy Spirit inform us we have to all agree with this idea. Even those who seem to hate themselves are in fact living in a selfishness that stems from their resentment of not being as good as they selfishly think they should be or not being where they selfishly think they could be. So even self-hate is selfishness at its core. The truth is that selfishness is the root of all of our inability to love others no matter how much we insist it isn't.

In a house of grace, love shows no favorites among family members, or else it rejects the words of Christ. But love according to Jesus must come from loving God with 100% of our hearts. That means that there might be times when an emotionally needy child comes before a spouse. In this instance, love is discerning and grace-filled. And in this instance, a child doesn't feel like a second-class citizen sacrificed on the altar of parental "needs" or romantic priorities.

This refusal to prioritize members of the family over one another is seen when you refuse to agree with your spouse when their choice is sinful. When a spouse is acting in an unloving or ungodly way it is unloving for us to stand in agreement with them simply because of our slogan "spouse second and child third." When we make this worldly slogan our precept for life we oftentimes are forced to choose it over God's Word itself, and in this we reject grace in favor of man-made law.

In a home where the spouse takes priority over the children, grace is in limited supply for our kids because our spouse gets the largest portion. This doesn't go unnoticed. In these moments, what they see is hypocrisy and unkindness, as grace is rejected in favor of favoritism and status. Anytime we side with someone because they are our chosen or our covenantal favorite we put someone else in between us and God. In his acclaimed devotional, My Utmost for His Highest, Oswald Chambers, until now, has been a lone voice crying out,

*"Your priorities must be God first, God second, and God third, until your life is continually face to face with God and no one else is taken into account whatsoever. Your prayer will then be, "In all the world there is no one but You, dear God; there is no one but You."*

When a parent utters these words, "there is no one but you, dear God," a child sees the power of a God who deserves that kind of true devotion. When out of that devotion comes impartial love for everyone, they see what love truly is. And they experience love as it was meant to be experienced, born out of complete devotion to love Himself.

Until we get this idea and reject playing favorites, our children will find it hard to devote their entire hearts to our God, but instead will look to another human to fill that part they see they are lacking from the very ones who were meant to share the depth of God's love with them. When we fail to share His love equally we, like the UPS man who takes some of the packages home for himself every night rather than deliver them, serve ourselves and fail to give others what they rightly deserve.

## Conclusion

Change shows progress. And as we build this house of grace we are continually a work in progress; we will not arrive until we see him face to face. So we cannot let our fear of change or of the unknown distract us from the calling of discipling our children into a growing relationship with the Father. And in this process of building it is essential that we learn to build a faith that will one day belong to our children, one that they will make their own. The tough news with this idea is that in order to do that our faith must be authentic because our kids will not adopt a faith that we teach but do not own. Going to church is not owning your faith. Forcing compliance to rules or a lifestyle you don't live up to yourself is not owning your faith. The idea that somehow our kids will adopt a faith that we have not adopted is kindness misplaced and insanity. The greatest kindness we could do our children is to have an authentic faith of our own, that they learn through imitation and receiving the fruit of our faith, not offering them one that we cannot claim as our own.

How you love and disciple your kids helps establish the foundation for the character of God to that child. Are you showing them a kind and gracious God who is patient beyond measure and merciful beyond belief? Have you shown them the grace of God to the level that he has shown it to you? Your acceptance of His grace prepares you to do just that. Remembering that you don't deserve to be alive should feed your soul and inform your interaction as a parent. Kids learn the most by observation not dictation, in conversation not lecture. As they observe and interact with God's grace alive in you it becomes real to them.

As you finish this book, I know I have left out a lot of questions and answers. After all, if every child, parent, family, and situation is different, well, that's a lot of scenarios! Let me just say, I have messed up spectacularly in my life and that includes parenting. But just like in the introduction, our goal as parents and Christians should be to learn how to rebound from failure. God's grace is big enough for us as parents. If you have more questions, I hope you jump online and head over to www.gracecity.org where we build a community of families that want to mute harshness and amplify grace in our homes.

My closing prayer is this: that you the reader have begun to process and consider what it is to build a house of grace. That when we build a house of grace from the wood gathered from branches that have been living apart from the vine, earthly wisdom, or even biblical wisdom detached from the gospel, the house will rot and eventually fall or merely stand tall as a testament to something other than the gospel. But when we build it from the wood of the living vine, that wood never rots or grows brittle. It is continually renewed and strengthened by the Holy Spirit. Built from this wood, we find a home that is ever growing, constructed shoulder-to-shoulder through discipleship, held together with the fruit of the Spirit, and covered in his love and grace.

* * *

More *House of Grace* content at:

# GRACECITY.ORG

# ABOUT THE AUTHOR

Michael DiMarco has sinned spectacularly in his personal and professional life. A life-long gambler turned ordained minister, he is working to reach the lost in the Bible Belt and other "christiany" cultures as a missionary to the "reached;" he speaks and writes to those that have missed the point of the gospel, been hurt by the church, or want to be freed from moralism.

A multitasker at heart, besides being a sinner, he also runs Hungry Planet, an independent publishing imprint and communications company that's produced over 40 books and sold 1.4 million copies worldwide.

His books include *Die Young, Own It, Independence Day, God Guy, Devotions for the God Guy*, the *God Guy Devotional Bible*, and the 2010 Christian Book of the Year for Youth- *Before You Date*. He is married to another bestselling author, Hayley DiMarco, and is father to the test subject of this book. Originally from Oregon (#GoDucks), the family lives on the shores of Old Hickory Lake just outside of Nashville, Tennessee.

His background includes a degree in mass communication, hosting talk radio, coaching volleyball at the university level, working as a teacher/presenter at the largest Bible software company in the world, minister to young adults at a large church in Nashville, and stints as a marketing and creative strategist for some of the largest organizations and ministries around.

# ABOUT HUNGRY PLANET

"Hungry Planet consistently creates messages and books that connect with students and their parents, tackle the toughest topics that they face, and they pull no punches in offering authentic, and oftentimes hard truth that readers need to hear."

Dr. Jim Burns, PhD. - Founder of HomeWord (formerly YouthBuilders) and author of *Creating an Intimate Marriage* and *Confident Parenting*

"Recently I was planning an off-site leadership retreat for our ministry and needed just the right voice to swoop in, understand our culture, speak into our souls and spark engaging and thoughtful conversation. I called Michael DiMarco at Hungry Planet. Michael has the unique gift of being able to discern cultural nuances while being able to ask difficult questions in a disarming way. The manner in which he facilitates strategic conversations communicates to me that he's a leader who is striving to place his finger on the pulse of what God is up to in a culture that's running counter to that same pursuit."

Matt Markins - Executive Director of Ministry Resources,
Vice President of Marketing and Strategy - Awana®

Hungry Planet has been "Feeding the World's Appetite for Truth" with twenty-four CBA bestsellers, 1.4 million copies sold, six ECPA Christian Book Award finalists (two winners,) consulting for Catalyst, Teen Mania, and Barna Research, speakers for Precept, MOPS, D6, LifeWay Students, FUGE Camps, and Women of Faith, frequent guests on Family Life Today, HomeWord, 100 Huntley Street, The 700 Club, , Moody Radio, and others.

Contact us for your publishing, consulting, speaking, or media needs at: www.hungryplanet.net

# ACKNOWLEDGMENTS

Ben & Kiersten Williams, Jordan & Lori Mycoskie, Mark Brasfield, Seth Kiehl, Gwen Smith, Jonathan Elder, Kristin Blair, and Renae McLeary. Your belief in this book and help to make it happen was inspiring. Thank you.

Diane Schassen, Karen Koch, La Chel Carson, Randy Shepard, Kim Bair, Beth Lockamy, Anita Gentry, Misty Benz, and Michele Bannister, thank you for your proofreading efforts under a tight deadline. Anything missed in this book is my fault! Your words of encouragement got me through my least favorite part of publishing.

Pastor Raymond Vogtner at Faith Church in Mount Juliet, TN and Children's Pastor Chad Smith at First Baptist Jacksonville, you allowed me access to your buildings and people as test kitchens and first victims for my four-week *House of Grace* series before the book was done. I was and am humbled at your invitation, trust, and friendship. I am in your debt.

Pete Sutton at Christ Community Church in St. Charles, IL, Greg Joiner at Fellowship Bible Church in Brentwood, TN, and all the other youth pastors that allowed me to "tack on" a parents' session at the end of your youth events for my Building a Culture of Confession talk, thank you. The positive feedback from those opportunities helped birth this book.

Paul Turner, thank you for friendship and listening to my rant on confession in Panera years ago. The opportunity to present the first and less rantish version to student ministers and youth workers at LifeWay was catalytic. Ron Hunter at D6, and Matt Markins at AWANA, you too were instrumental in giving me opportunities to present portions of this message in front of pastors and influencers. Thank you for your friendship and support.

To all my friends in Christian publishing, thank you for all the lessons you've taught me. Sorry I was sometimes a bull in a china shop. To Christian retailers, you are your community's spiritual walk-in clinic Mon.-Sat. Thank you for selling our particular brand of medicine!

Greg, Johnny, and Harry, I miss our Chik-fil-a Mondays. Come back!

You all know who you are; I wish there were do overs.

Mom & Dad, I miss you. I wish you could know my girls.

Addy, I love you no matter what.

Hayley, we did it.

# MORE BOOKS FROM HUNGRY PLANET

*God Guy: Becoming the Man You Were Meant to Be*

*Devotions for the God Guy: A 365-Day Journey*

*God Guy Devotional Bible (ESV, & GWT translations)*

*God Girl: Becoming the Woman You Were Meant to Be*

*Devotions for the God Girl: A 365-Day Journey*

*God Girl Devotional Bible (ESV, GWT, & NKJV translations)*

*The Fruitful Wife: Cultivating a Love Only God Can Produce*

*Die Young: Burying Your Self In Christ*

*Obsessed: Breaking Free From the Things That Consume You*

*Obsessed (Bible Study): Making Christ the Desire of Your Heart*

*Own It: Leaving Behind a Borrowed Faith*

*The Big Picture: Making God the Main Focus of Your Life*

*Before You Date: Seven Things You Must Know Before You Go*

*All In: Gambling on Life, Love, and Faith in a World of Risk*

*Independence Day: Graduating into a New World of Freedom, Temptation, and Opportunity*

See the entire title list at www.hungryplanet.net

# ENDNOTES

i. *Disciple*, Bill Clem, p. 137 Crossway, Wheaton

ii. *Treasury of David, All of Grace*, Charles Spurgeon

iii. Maccoby, EE and Martin, JA. (1983). Socialization in the context of the family: Parent-child interaction. In P Mussen and EM Hetherington, editors, *Handbook of Child Psychology*, volume IV: Socialization, personality, and social development, chapter 1, pages 1-101. New York: Wiley, 4th edition

iv. http://news.byu.edu/archive10-jun-parentingstyle.aspx

v. http://news.byu.edu/archive10-jun-parentingstyle.aspx

vi *Journal of Studies on Alcohol and Drugs*, Stephen J. Bahr, John P. Hoffmann, Vol. 71, 2010, Issue 4, July 2010, State University of New Jersey, Rutgers.

vii. *Spiritual Disciplines, Spiritual Formation and the Restoration of the Soul*, Dallas Willard. Journal of Psychology and Theology, Spring 1998, Vol. 26, #1, pp. 101-109

viii. *Treasury of David, All of Grace*, Charles Spurgeon

ix. *My Utmost for His Highest*, Oswald Chambers, May 8th.

x. *New Bible Commentary*, ed. D. A. Carson: 21st Century Edition, 4th ed., 1 Jn 5:1-5 (Leicester, England; Downers Grove, Ill., USA: Inter-Varsity Press, 1994).

xi. *Nelson's New Illustrated Bible Dictionary*, ed. Ronald F. Youngblood, F. F. Bruce, R. K. Harrison and Thomas Nelson Publishers (Nashville, TN: Thomas Nelson, Inc., 1995).

xii. *Own It*, Michael & Hayley DiMarco, B&H, Nashville

xiii. *Own It*, Michael & Hayley DiMarco, B&H, Nashville

CPSIA information can be obtained at www.ICGtesting.com
Printed in the USA
LVOW11s1258080215

425944LV00007B/12/P

9 780986 134906